A Journey into Strategy

A Journey into Strategy

LESSONS IN LEADERSHIP AND LIFE

Ray Melleady

CHESTER SPRINGS

PENNSYLVANIA

2017

Contents

Acknowledgments

THIS BOOK NEVER could have been written without the help of some important and influential people in my life. I am indebted to all of them for their encouragement, support, inspiration, and ideas.

Specifically, I wish to express my sincerest thanks to the following:

- ◇ My wife, Shannon, for putting up with my unusual work habits and for creating a beautiful family with me.

- ◇ My children—Dan, Matt, Kellie, Connor, and Ian—for their love, for their caring for each other, and for making me a responsible adult at a relatively early age. Be magnanimous always. *Te quiero mas que me vida.*

- ◇ My parents, John and Judy Melleady, for giving their children so much when they had so little, for instilling in me the discipline to think with an open mind, to see things forward, and always to give more than I take.

- Luther Diggs and Steve Bland, for giving a young man with little formal education an opportunity to prove himself and, eventually, to get that education. Luther made me a supervisor at the age of 21 and put me in one of the toughest union shops in Philadelphia, where he knew that succeeding would be a challenge but would jump-start my career. Steve made me a chief operating officer before I had the required college degree, and allowed me to finish the degree while I "stirred the pot" in Albany, NY. My mind is remarkably different for having worked for both of them.
- Christian Hammarskjold, for sharing his unique mind at a pivotal point in my career and for allowing me to earn an equity position in his firm.
- Tom Bramante, for his valuable and timely advice and leadership in the early stages of my management career.
- The management team at the SEPTA Berridge Facility, for being a part of that organization's (and my personal) transformation and being so much a part of how I think today.
- Mark Aesch, for pushing me to write this book and making his unique strategic mind available as a resource in that effort.
- Art Fischman, for helping me to structure my ideas and translate often-complex concepts into clear, efficient language, and for keeping me on track from first page to last.

A Journey into Strategy

Introduction

YOU CAN LEARN a lot being around buses and trains.

I began that phase of my education as a technician with SEPTA (Southeastern Pennsylvania Transportation Authority) in 1987. Right out of high school, I went to work in the transit industry, fueling and cleaning buses at night in North Philadelphia. I aspired to be a diesel technician, and union rules required that I start at an entry-level position. I learned frontline operations as a technician for several years, then moved up to shop foreman, then plant manager, then technical instructor. After two years as foreman with New Jersey Transit, I returned to SEPTA as director of maintenance.

Director of maintenance for SEPTA—not bad, considering where I had started my journey through life. My father was a bus driver, first with the Philadelphia Transportation Company and then with SEPTA. He worked holidays and weekends and lots of odd shifts while I was growing up in a row home on East Thayer Street in North Philadelphia's blue-collar Kensington section. I got through high school but couldn't afford college because I had a baby to feed. In fact, by the time I was 25 my wife and I had three little mouths to feed. But even if I could have afforded it, I didn't see any reason for going to college back then. After all, didn't I already know everything I needed to know?

Two things I did know about were sacrifice and responsibility; having three children at the age of 25 can do that for you. And so, in spite of—or perhaps *because* of—the challenges confronting me on the home front, I continued to immerse myself completely in my work, learning everything I could to qualify for positions of greater responsibility. In 2006 I began serving as executive director of the Capital District Transportation Authority in Albany, New York. By 2008 I was also president and board chair of the New York Public Transit Association.

For me, the American Dream was alive and well, and I was using public transportation to get there.

I suppose I could have written a book about public transportation, but this is surely not that book. This is a book about business leadership and how everything—or almost everything—you need to know to be an effective business leader can be learned from studying how transit systems operate.

Today I'm managing director of North American operations for a private corporation, where I am responsible for a pipeline of business opportunities valued at more than $100 million in annual revenue. Much of my success I attribute to what I've learned about transportation over many years. Much of it, that is, but not all of it. What transit systems taught me about the principles of business leadership also deserves a lot of the credit.

Where I *haven't* learned all that much is from books on management and leadership, and I've read hundreds of them. Quite a few miss the mark, having been written from an academic perspective, with no "real-life" content to speak of. Or, worse, they overcomplicate the role that leadership plays in a successful business. News flash: Organizations aren't loyal; *people* are loyal. They work hard for leaders whom they trust and respect.

Many organizations miss the mark as well, reacting to individual events instead of anticipating patterns of activity that are characteristic of specific industries and of businesses in general. When organizations respond to an adverse event—whether it be a bad quarter, a bad economy, or a bad executive hiring decision—more often than not they fail to identify and address the root cause of the challenge they face.

Most leadership principles come under the heading of common sense, but people don't or won't believe that: *don't*, because they don't believe it can be that simple, or *won't*, because if it's really as simple as it sounds, why do we have so many experts out there trying to tell us what it really means? In my experience, it's not the complicated things that get missed in a position of leadership; it's the simple things. For example: [1]

◇ Developing a clear and concise vision and communicating it to stakeholders on whom it will have an impact.

◇ Recognizing and accepting your current reality.

◇ Developing a strategic plan that outlines requirements, responsibilities, and timing to close the gap between today's reality and the future desired state.

In my opinion, it's not much more complex than that. The "science" of business leadership can be as simple as reading a transit map, as understanding a schedule, as planning a trip. As easy as understanding what leaves riders satisfied or dissatisfied and employees engaged.

At this stage in my career, I've come to understand what makes for an effective transit system—a system that runs on time, provides good connections, is efficient, gets the most out of its employees, and delivers the best service to its customers.

As a senior executive in a business organization, I've also become aware of several parallels between effective transportation systems and smoothly running, profitable companies. The similarities are striking and, more important, a lot easier to grasp than the managerial and leadership "secrets" touted in the latest business bestsellers.

In fact, I've identified nine attributes of successful transportation systems that can be mapped directly onto almost any business organization. They are shown in tabular form in Table 1.

In the chapters that follow, we'll take a close look at how transit systems run, why they succeed, what we can learn from their success, and how those lessons can be applied to running any business, as well as to how we conduct our personal lives.

In business, acting or reacting "out of context" is a sure recipe for failure. No challenge exists in isolation, just as no solution has consequences limited only to its immediate corner of the organization. My hope in writing this book is to provide business leaders and aspiring leaders a convenient paradigm for seeing and remembering the essential attributes and patterns of effective leadership and, when it comes time to act, for choosing an alternative consistent with the character and mission of the organization.

Table 1. Attributes of Successful Transportation Systems That Apply to Almost Any Business Organization

	Transit System	**Business Organization**
Trip Planning	Determining the most likely path for riders to get from Point A to Point B successfully and efficiently.	Determining and effectively articulating a clear and concise business vision and purpose for the organization.
Structure	Building an infrastructure with the full realization that a transportation system can only ever be as good as the roads or tracks on which it runs.	Building an organizational hierarchy that will determine the effectiveness with which strategy is decided and executed, and that will ultimately limit the organization or make it better.
Making Connections	Coordinating nodes within the system to get riders from Point A to Point B with maximum efficiency and the excellent mobility made possible by seamless connections.	Ensuring a clearly developed network of stakeholders and a maintenance relationship strategy to develop positive equity in key relationships that can help to convert vision to reality.
Time Management	Managing schedules both on and off peak to ensure optimal asset utilization and on-time departures and arrivals.	Determining priorities and managing them through peak and off-peak performance times (downtime) to ensure that projects requiring the most time receive it.
Strategic Planning	Determining how shifts in travel patterns, population centers, and other factors will create new requirements for satisfying riders.	Looking beyond today's challenges toward the possibilities of the future generated by changes in the economy, technology, and the marketplace, among others, and providing a blueprint for progress and a shared perspective.
Execution	"Moving the chains" to get things done by overcoming the resistance of those committed to the status quo.	Enlisting the aid of stakeholders and employees required to turn a vision, as captured within a strategic plan, into a tangible reality.

(continued on next page)

Table 1 *(continued)*

	Transit System	Business Organization
Accountability	Creating expectations for system performance and meting out consequences, both good and bad, depending on outcomes measured using key metrics.	Creating expectations and consequences, for yourself and others, that attach to all facets of job performance and, measured against key metrics, determine the altitude to which one climbs on the org chart.
Change Management	Communicating with unions, riders, and the general public to ensure that neither internal nor external changes adversely affect customer service delivery or quality.	Creating the trust needed to foster positive conflict, without which there can be no change and no progress. It's about creating an environment where people feel comfortable with disagreement.
Equity	Ensuring that your transit system is structured in such a manner that all citizens have equal access to mobility options.	Aligning people's natural attributes and skills with appropriate jobs and training programs, and developing clearly defined career ladders to offer fair and equitable promotional opportunities to every employee.

CHAPTER 1

Trip Planning and Finding Your Destination

The simple act of planning a trip involves the same thought processes as creating a vision for your business or personal life. Planning a trip to a meeting is not unlike planning your trip in life; it's something you need to do if you're going to have any hope of reaching your destination.

Well, it's a winding road
When you're in the lost and found.
—Zac Brown Band

PLANNING A TRIP—it's something we all do. Whether it's getting to work during rush hour, mapping out the best route to hit the high spots on a journey down the coast, or figuring out the multiple legs of an international flight, we would never think of leaving home without having some idea of how we're going to get to where we're going.

But not all trips involve wheels or wings. Call me obsessive, but I've spent a lot of time planning my own trip through life. And (while you're at it) call me irrational, but I knew at the age of 20, having barely made it through high school to spend my days turning wrenches as a diesel technician, that I was going to be the CEO of a major transit system before the age of 40. I had no connections, no prospects for getting a college degree, and no management or governmental affairs experience. But vision is not under the control of the rational mind. In some respects, vision is directly at odds with the rational mind—you know, the rational mind that tells you, in no uncertain terms, what you can and cannot do. Vision doesn't worry about what you can and cannot do. Vision conveys what you *will be*, irrespective of your current circumstances. So be careful about what you expect; we have learned that the mind can and will attract the circumstances that fulfill your expectations.

I even plotted my steps (or stops) along the way, which included being a director of maintenance by 30 and a chief operating officer by 35. I just let my subconscious in on my trip plan, set it to autopilot, and then got out of the way. My subconscious seemed to know everything I needed to do to become a CEO—things such as gaining experience, developing key stakeholders, and getting an education.

Executing a trip plan is something that companies can do as well, with organizational culture playing the role of a collective subconscious. When corporate vision becomes ingrained in corporate culture, great things can happen.

At the risk of stating the obvious, transit systems—not just their riders—need to do some trip planning as well (with "trip planning" here representing the transit-system version of vision). Whatever the vision of a transit system may be—whether to decrease a regional carbon footprint by X, to increase its modal share of ridership, to be the leading transportation option in your region, or to achieve an improved quality of life in your region—an organizational trip plan is required to map out a path to that "destination." The trip planning (or vision) undertaken by a transit system is more complex than the kind to which you may be accustomed. It requires incredible foresight to envision future travel patterns and infrastructure requirements that are 15 or 20 years beyond what we have today. This is because allocation decisions need to be made far in advance of actual outcomes; those benefiting or otherwise affected are rarely aware of the vision required and the battles fought to secure a firm direction. Such decisions also require extensive stakeholder outreach and buy-in—something I will speak to at length in a later chapter.

Like most CEOs in the transit industry, I was working from a painted canvas. The highways and roadways in the region where I worked had already been established, and the result was a move away from cities and into the suburbs. People were in search of cheaper land, and with that came longer commutes. In the United States, land was a blessing and a curse. Once we entered the automotive age, we mistakenly believed that we no longer needed transit and moved from vertical to horizontal development patterns. Suburban sprawl dominated the landscape. For the most part, highways were built for the movement of cars and trucks, not people and goods. Economically, our infrastructure was designed and built on $30-per-barrel oil, with a blind eye to the environment. And yet, a CEO must see beyond current circumstances and envision a preferred future state; current circumstances may have nothing to do with future realities. This is not to suggest that CEOs ignore current circumstances—only that they need to be far more strategic than tactical. As a CEO in transit or in business, it's your job to see it, believe it, and sell it—to repaint the canvas in a meaningful way. A transit system's vision may describe access to future employment centers, modify travel patterns, and increase ridership potential, and is the result of a series of questions that, in any corporation, might fall under the heading of *What we need to know to satisfy our customers*. In the case of transit systems, the needed information could include any or all of the following:

◇ Where do riders need to go and at what hours?
◇ How might riders' destinations change over time due to shifts in population centers or industrial corridors?
◇ How do we attract the customer of the future?
◇ For that matter, how do we attract the employee of the future?
◇ What about resource availability, including identifying real estate and air rights that are available for surface, underground, or elevated travel corridors, and how it might best be utilized?
◇ In the case of surface transit, what about the potential impact on existing traffic patterns? Will added convenience for some commuters result in increased inconvenience for others?
◇ How can we best connect with new and future mobility technologies and providers (think Uber and automated vehicles)?
◇ What other patterns are at work here that might help us see what's likely to happen in the future?

All of these questions must be considered when you try to plan for riders' transportation demands both now and in the future. And, in my experience, during the process of developing a bold picture of the future you're likely to find many voices of counsel and few voices of vision.

You're likely to find many voices of counsel and few voices of vision.

Vision can transform the future incrementally. The Futures Cone developed by Clem Bezold (Figure 1) illustrates the various types of futures that can be charted in the

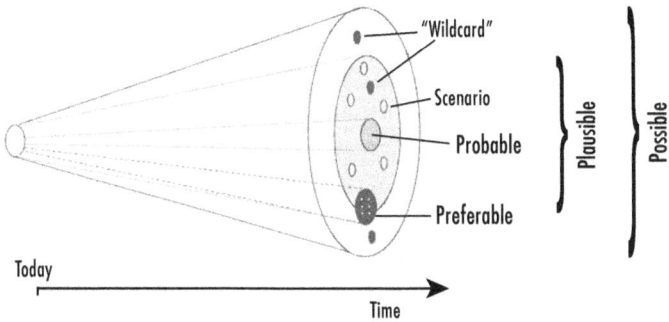

Figure 1. Types of futures—the Futures Cone developed by Clem Bezold

human mind. These include futures that are possible, plausible, preferable, and/or probable. I believe that you need to be aware of what's possible and plausible to sort out what you want to achieve from what you want to avoid, but your vision ought to steer the organization or yourself toward a preferred future state. In doing so, you develop a gap between your current and future state which, when communicated correctly, generates the creative tension that transforms an individual, a group, and an organization.

Money should not govern vision. Do not pursue money. Pursue vision and purpose, and let money pursue you. Life is about perspective, not circumstance.

> Money should not govern vision.

In both the limited context of a literal journey and the much broader context of a metaphorical journey—a career or a political campaign, for example—a trip plan is the outcome of a vision. A route plan is one of several pieces that make up a transit system's vision. When I was at the Capital District Transportation Authority (CDTA) in Albany, New York, one of my objectives was to integrate transportation with land-use patterns, and our routes were designed to accommodate that objective. Our vision was to be a premier transportation provider—a provider of choice. New route development was an outcome of that vision.

Clearly transit systems plan more effectively when they use as a starting point an unobstructed view of where they want to be in the future and then work their way backward to the present. This is a trip plan that's not measured in minutes or hours but in years and sometimes decades.

. . . a trip plan that's not measured in minutes or hours but in years and sometimes decades.

When I write about vision, I should also speak to the inevitable outcome accompanying the absence of vision. There are currently cities in the United States that come to a standstill twice every day because, 70 years ago, planners undervalued the impact of mass transportation or, said another way, they focused on the movement of cars and trucks instead of the movement of people. They encouraged the single-occupant vehicle, rather than mass transit, for moving people, and similarly relied on highways, not rail, to move freight. Lobbyists for the oil companies and auto manufacturers went around DC advocating for investments for more highways, more asphalt, more lanes, and fewer rails. In the past decade people finally came to recognize that this was unsustainable; we can no longer maintain what was already built, much less accommodate new vehicles. In other words, transportation planners and key stakeholders failed to plan their trip. As a result, commuters in these cities pay a heavy tax on the most valued of currencies—time. According to the Texas Transit Institute, in 2014 congestion caused urban Americans to travel an extra 6.9 billion hours and purchase an extra 3.1 billion gallons of fuel for a congestion cost of $160 billion. Moreover, automotive travel is the least-safe travel option in the United States, with tens of thousands of people dying each year in passenger cars, motorcycles, and trucks, according to the

Eno Foundation. These aren't empty stats; they are a deliberate outcome of the absence of national vision for mobility. The absence of vision has a cost.

The absence of vision has a cost.

Despite today's clear reality, we still have many short-sighted politicians who refuse to support adequate funding of transportation programs under the guise of espousing a "no new taxes" position. They fail to understand that to withhold funding is to ensure congestion and effectively to levy a "time tax" on all commuters, relegating them—whether in a car or on a bus—to be stuck in traffic twice a day, every day. It is a tax unfairly imposed on future generations as well.

In my travels, I have found that one of the primary differences between highly civilized societies and those less civilized is access to mobility. Meaningful mobility planning provides us with better access to jobs, reduced congestion, social equity, reduced emissions, and energy independence (don't get me started), but it also helps to ensure that future generations won't get stuck in traffic. It ensures our children and grandchildren an improved quality of life. It also ensures the economic vitality of a region, with those regions choked in traffic becoming destined to lose economic competitiveness. In the future, companies and people will choose to locate and live in areas that have access to safe, convenient, high-tech mobility options. Regions that ignore this reality and fail to make needed investments in transportation infrastructure and mobility are going to lose. You can listen to me now or believe me later.

It's no different for any business. Every organization that has customers and hopes to succeed needs to begin by acknowledging where it is now and where it would like to be in five years or ten years. I have found that the customer is the best filter for just about every business decision you make. So why are most companies structured to make life better for the agency, not the customer? The business (that is to say, its leadership) needs to plan its trip into the future, finding the most efficient way to get to where it wants to go. That means thinking about the same kinds of issues that transit companies face in trying to meet current customer demands and anticipate future needs.

VISION

So, it's "the vision thing," I can hear you say to yourself. Vision, mission, purpose, goals, special sauce, and all those other headings that get written on large pieces of paper and taped to the wall at that corporate retreat you're required to attend every year. That's what we're talking about here, isn't it? Well, yes, but organizational "trip planning" is more than that. As with a real trip plan, it's something that needs to include every stop along the way—from annual goals and quarterly objectives to every ad campaign and product launch and executive recruitment initiative you undertake. And every time you reorganize, whether it's a single department or an entire corporation, you need to think long-term and then work backward to the present. What does the marketplace need and want right now? What will it need and want in the future? How is this organization positioned now (Point A) and where will it be in the future (Point B) to capitalize on this movement? And, given the above data, what is the most effective and efficient route from Point A to Point B?

I think of trip planning as "vision +." Yes, it is a destination, but, as with any trip, it's all about the journey. (Someone once said "obstacles are those frightful things you see when you take your eyes off the goal.") A trip may require a planned or unplanned layover, a detour, or a timing risk—

for example, the possibility of not getting to an intermediate stop in time to make a connection. For a business's vision, the same considerations apply: long-term vision, goals, interim objectives, capital (including human capital), and unforeseen events, among others. All must be factored into the organizational trip plan.

Vision needs to be defined precisely and used in context if it's going to have any value in business planning. Adopting another company's purpose or vision solely because that other company is more successful than your company is not a good trip plan. Success comes in many flavors, and, while the "let's-do-what-they're-doing" vision may make sense if it reflects the direction in which the marketplace is moving, organizational vision needs to be based on more than a wish. If a transit system based its routes and terminals and schedules on someone's wish, you might have a problem. You, the rider, that is. Just as a transit system needs to reflect the preferences of its customers, *any* business is all about serving customers, and any plan for the future that's adopted—any vision chosen as a rallying cry for the organization—needs to be about what customers are looking for now and, more important, will be looking for in the future.

PURPOSE VS. VISION

Before going further, I'd like to draw a simple distinction between purpose (or mission) and vision. I have always found it useful to think of purpose as an organization's external aspiration, and vision as its internal aspiration. A company's purpose could be to build computers, to stage large events, to market organic produce, to provide a low-cost local transportation alternative, and so on. Purpose is, in its most fundamental form, what we do for our customers—it's why we went into business in the first place. It needs to be easy to remember and to resonate with people in the organization. That's because people don't commit to plans—they commit to purpose. It can be modified over time, especially as advances in technology and changes in other external factors render a company's original purpose obsolete. For example, a company that entered the marketplace to provide the fastest and highest quality fax transmissions available anywhere would be well advised to update that purpose to reflect how people are currently using document-transmission technology or, even better, how they will be using it in the future. But, in any case, an organization's stated purpose cannot be simply to make a lot of money (although that's exactly why most people start businesses) because no customer or employee is going to respond favorably to that purpose alone, and our purpose is what we rely on initially to inspire employees and bring us customers.

Every business exists to fill some need, and defining a business's purpose begins with assessing what needs exist to be filled. In the case of a transit system, we're focusing largely on the needs of prospective riders: What are their likely destinations? What expectations do they have regarding time, cost, and convenience, including on-board amenities, ease of purchasing tickets, availability of special rates, and the distance of terminals from those riders' likely destinations? A transit system's purpose may be simply to provide the transportation experience that riders want and expect. At CDTA in Albany, our stated purpose was to provide safe, reliable, and cost-effective transportation for the Capital Region. In business, we need to listen to what the market is telling us about which of their needs customers are most eager to see filled. If justified by the magnitude of the need, a business corporation's stated purpose may be no more than to provide customers with the tools they need (for software, gardening, whatever) at a reasonable price.

Vision, on the other hand, is what we hope to achieve for ourselves or, stated more resolutely, what we *will* achieve for ourselves—capture a 30 percent share in the PC market, be the market leader in organic produce, become a $3 billion company, and so forth. It is vision that sets the bar and, looking out five or ten years, answers the question: *What is the preferred future state of this company?* Yes, vision has a lot to do with our relationship with customers, but it is primarily about what *we* want to be to have greater appeal with customers and suppliers, and only secondarily what we are doing for customers. At times vision can ignore current customer sentiment. Sometimes customers don't know what they want until they see it. Is need the mother of all invention, or is invention the mother of all need? (Think iPhone.)

Is need the mother of all invention, or is invention the mother of all need?

A transit company's vision could include, for instance, attaining a certain level of modal market share, eventually getting the public to rely on this transit system as the primary means of travel in a particular region, or becoming the primary employer in that region, all of which accompany and contribute to that company's achieving its purpose of providing riders with a quality commuting experience. As for a corporation whose purpose is to provide its customers with great tools at a reasonable price, what needs to happen to fulfill that purpose? Must you achieve a 10 percent market share in five years? Or become a market leader? Must your brand become a household name? Must you have branches in 10 states? In 30 countries? Become a $3 billion company? A $10 billion company? Have 10,000 employees? All of these possible goals could factor into the company's vision as it goes about working toward its purpose.

Quite often, people mistakenly create a vision solely within the context of present circumstances, which typically include some kind of financial constraints. I appreciate as much as anyone the importance of completing a project within budget, but a vision limited from the outset by current financial realities is probably not a vision that's going to break new ground for your company. While I was CEO at CDTA, I worked with key stakeholders on a vision for 100 miles of bus rapid transit—a plan that would relieve congestion, stimulate the economy, improve air quality, and reshape mobility options for future generations. A noble vision, indeed, except that we were installing high-speed bus transit lines on top of rail lines that had, over the years, been buried under layers of asphalt. Our vision was essentially to turn infrastructure that was built to move people (rail lines) but converted to the movement of cars (asphalt) back to bus rapid transit lines for the movement of people. Talk about the past being prologue, or, perhaps in this case, a bit more than prologue. We had forgotten what our fathers taught us.

At the time we created this vision, there was no money available to support it, which meant we had on our hands that most deadly of creatures, the "unfunded vision." But that was fine with me. You see, once you bring dollars and cents into a creative brainstorming session, you're effectively imposing significant restrictions on the group's creativity. As far as I'm concerned, *all* visions should be unfunded. In my experience, there is more money in search of vision than vision in search of money.

There is more money in search of vision than vision in search of money.

And sure enough, when we communicated the CDTA vision to a broader group of stakeholders, we had no trouble generating funding options. We engaged the community, which bought into and further developed the vision. We helped business members understand how this investment would help them improve access to jobs and create new opportunities for growth. And, ultimately, we garnered a broad base of political support for the vision. With funding programs identified, we were able to advance the project. *A strong vision supported by the appropriate stakeholder group will always find creative capital.* Had we put off our "trip planning" until funding was available, we would never have left the office. Vision begets funding, not the other way around. Vision also needs to engage the workforce and key stakeholders so that the collective subconscious (that is, the culture of the organization) can guide the trip.

As I've noted, I like to think of vision as a preferred future state of being. When you create a vision, you are, in effect, seeding the individual or corporate subconscious with a future state and allowing it to work toward that outcome. We human beings are goal-driven creatures. Most often our problem is not that we cannot attain our goals, but rather that we don't have any goals to attain. Or, looked at in another way, instead of doing something that will eventually enable us to redefine ourselves (for example, as "market leader"), why not create a vision that *begins* by redefining us? If the subconscious is as unsophisticated about tenses as I think it is, everything that enters it is probably in the present tense. So when we say that *we will be* the market leader, what our subconscious hears is, *we are* the market leader. We then let the power of suggestion drive our subconscious (and ourselves) to do whatever that redefinition requires. I know from personal experience that when it comes to planning your trip in life, you have only two options: Either vision will alter certainty, or certainty will alter vision. So plan your future, before your future plans you.

> Either vision will alter certainty, or certainty will alter vision.

DIRECTION (AKA ALIGNMENT)

The last element I want to talk about in connection with trip planning is direction. Let's begin again with the obvious: A transit system doesn't build all east-west routes if its purpose is to give riders a convenient means of traveling north and south. It also doesn't randomly add and remove stops every day on a particular route. Riders need predictability in their travel experience, and that predictability begins with directional logic and consistency. Similarly, a business needs to act in a manner consistent with its purpose and vision. For example, a computer corporation that aspires to become a premier services provider cannot continue compensating its sales reps at a higher rate for selling hardware than for selling services. If it does, it will always be a hardware company, no matter what its vision may be. Again, direction must be consistent with purpose and vision.

Direction is also about organizational alignment. For a leader, alignment means connecting the dots so that *all* people in the organization can clearly see their roles, as well as how those roles connect to the purpose and vision of the organization. As CEO at CDTA, my job was to transform vision into an operational reality. This meant communicating with people so that they understood how what they did was important to advancing the objectives of the organization. And this required that people be able to connect their own job objectives directly with departmental and organizational objectives. If a serviceperson on the fuel lane failed to perform a proper visual inspection and nightly service of a vehicle, the result could have been a breakdown that might in turn have resulted in someone's being late for work or for an appointment. The people we were transporting— our customers—were depending on us to get them to where they needed to go, and to get them there safely and on time. *Everyone* in the organization needed to feel that.

Alignment is what connects our short-term objectives with the company we want to be over the long term. And, by short-term, I mean not only quarterly and annual objectives but daily objectives as well. As far as riders are concerned, a transit system is only as good as its last rush-hour performance. Do the peak hours bring everything to a grinding halt, or is the system able to handle peak demand? Is it any different for the customers of any business? Does anyone seriously doubt that five years of customer satisfaction could be wiped out in a single 90-second phone call with a rude or unaccommodating customer service rep? Every business needs to ensure that its short-term objectives are consistent with its long-term vision. Making vision a reality starts with assuming the appropriate organizational alignment for that vision.

Direction is driven by performance measurement. When an organization communicates key measurements with which to define organizational success, people tend to pull in the same direction. Without those measurements, people are far more likely to work against each other. Having done a fair amount of international peer-group reviews, I'm not terribly fond of sports analogies (which often don't travel well), but think about what would happen if an NFL lineman didn't know what the next play was going to be. Should he fall back to protect the quarterback? Lead the blocking on an end run? Let the defender through in order to set up a screen pass? My point here is, it isn't even a matter of choosing between individual action and team-directed action. Without knowing what *the team* is planning to do, there's no way to know what *you're* supposed to do. As a leader, be clear about direction and individual contribution to the collective vision.

In the next chapter, we'll take a closer look at alignment in connection with the role of structure in transit systems, business organizations, and life.

SUMMARY

✓ In a transit system, in a corporation, and in our personal lives, trip planning is essential to getting to where you want to go, and getting there efficiently, not by default but by design. Plan your trip!

✓ For a business, satisfying customers is an important—usually the *most* important—requirement for achieving the organizational vision. A transit system addresses that requirement by, among other things, providing its riders with options to be used as the foundation for trip planning—getting from where they are to where they would like to be.

✓ *Purpose* or *mission* is what an organization does for its customers. It is why you exist. It can evolve over time.

✓ *Vision* is a future state that a business hopes to achieve to give that business greater appeal with customers and suppliers.

✓ When you create a vision, you are effectively redefining yourself because your subconscious (or, in business, the corporate culture) will interpret it as an accurate description of your current state of being and therefore work to bring reality in line with it.

✓ *Direction* must be consistent with purpose and vision and is driven by performance measurement. Organizational alignment is what connects short-term objectives with long-term vision, and frontline employees with purpose.

CHAPTER 2

Infrastructure and Structure

A transit system's infrastructure determines the relative mobility of its riders. A business organization's infrastructure (including how it is structured) sets parameters on the potential effectiveness of its people, their motivation to excel, and the extent to which they're able to contribute their talents and creativity toward achieving the organization's mission.

IN A TRANSIT system, infrastructure is everything; as in any business, this is where it all starts. A poor infrastructure can limit a region's mobility and economic development, no matter how much wisdom, knowledge, experience, and expertise are added later. Likewise, poor organizational structure can have a significant impact on communication, efficiency, and outcomes.

I'm often called on to work with agencies on their strategic planning process, an integral part of which is the identification of organizational strengths, weaknesses, opportunities, and challenges. More often than not, one of those weaknesses is poor communication, which I generally find to be symptomatic of a poorly structured organization. Frequent misdiagnosis—that is, attributing poor communication to some other, more immediately visible, condition—only compounds the problem. Whether you're stuck in traffic or in the office due to some obstacle to the flow of either information or people, an ineffective structure or infrastructure is often to blame.

THE COSTS OF POOR INFRASTRUCTURE

Good infrastructure means good access to mobility and future economic development. But perhaps the effects of poor infrastructure are easier to spot. When a bridge collapses, for example, people tend to notice. Take the collapse of the I-35W Mississippi River Bridge in Minneapolis in 2007, which killed 13 and injured 145. In 1990 and again in 2006, the federal government had rated the bridge "structurally deficient." An investigation determined the cause of the collapse to be a design flaw—steel gusset plates too small to support the increased load resulting from added concrete on the road surface along with almost 300 tons of construction equipment. A day after the collapse, Minnesota's Governor Tim Pawlenty said the bridge had been due for replacement in 2020.

According to an analysis of 2014 U.S. Department of Transportation data by the American Road & Transportation Builders Association, more than 61,000 U.S. bridges are now rated as structurally deficient, nearly nine in ten of which were built before 1970. Pennsylvania and Iowa each have more than 5,000 such bridges. With the Highway Trust Fund continuing to face revenue shortfalls, states are increasingly reluctant to make further transportation infrastructure investments.

Consider the case of the ill-fated Hudson River commuter train tunnel. In October 2010, New Jersey's Governor Chris Christie pulled the plug on what was then the nation's largest transit project, citing the recession and the likelihood of further cost overruns. In terminating the project, Christie forfeited his right to $3 billion of federal funding that had been earmarked for the tunnel. The new tunnel would have provided much needed additional capacity for traffic into Midtown Manhattan; rail access had been limited to two tunnels built in 1910. Political opponents claim that Christie intended to take the funds that New Jersey would have paid toward the tunnel project and redirect them toward the state's nearly bankrupt Transportation Trust Fund, thereby avoiding a politically suicidal tax increase on gasoline. A GAO audit found that New Jersey would not have paid 70 percent of the tunnel's cost, as Christie had claimed, but only 14.4 percent. Nor, as Christie had also claimed, had the estimate for cost overruns increased or would New Jersey be responsible for all overruns; the federal government had offered to share them.

The impact of all of this will be felt now and for years to come. Short-term agendas will always have long-term consequences. Rather than saving commuters money by avoiding an unwanted gas tax, Governor Christie has effectively levied a heavy "time tax" on everyone traveling between New York and New Jersey. As for the tunnel, it will be built someday; you can count on that. The only difference is, it will cost a lot more than it would have cost in 2010. You can count on that, too.

Short-term agendas will always have long-term consequences.

THE BENEFITS OF GOOD INFRASTRUCTURE

But enough (for now) about poor infrastructure. Let's talk about good infrastructure. Good structure in an organization is what enables effective communication and workflow.

Putting in place a good infrastructure requires tremendous foresight and brings benefits, many of which cannot be prefaced with dollar signs. Good infrastructure creates and maintains jobs, relieves congestion, provides access to jobs, increases real estate values, improves safety on our roadways, contributes to energy independence, improves air quality, creates options for mobility and emergency evacuation, and improves economic development. A poor infrastructure will do just the opposite across the board.

Put a well-designed train on poorly designed, inadequately maintained tracks and what you get is an unreliable train and a bad experience. As is the case with chains, an infrastructure is only as strong as its weakest link. Put a good train on good tracks but lay those tracks on bad railroad ties and, again, the result is service that is less than safe and less than reliable.

GOVERNANCE AND THE EVOLUTION OF STRUCTURE

Yes, a good structure is required for good performance, but structure alone does not guarantee good performance. For public sector agencies, organizational structure is generally governed by appointed or elected boards. These governing bodies have been developed through state and federal legislative actions over the course of decades; they exist to ensure that the organization carries out its purpose. Absent good governance, even a well-structured organization can underperform. Of course, absent a relevant structure, an organization *is certain to* underperform. Quite often performance is viewed as the problem, rather than as a symptom of bad structure.

But (comes the reply) no one would ever intentionally design a redundant, overlapping governance structure. Structure or governance, however, can evolve . . . and evolve badly; over time, this will result in less effective performance. New York State, for example, has 11 Department of Transportation (DOT) regions, 12 Metropolitan Planning Organizations (MPOs), and 35 transit systems, all with their own agendas and governing bodies. The system is naturally loaded with redundancies and restricted performance. Believe me, no one sat down and designed this structure from scratch. Rather, it was developed over a period of years in response to external conditions the same way you might sequentially build eight different additions onto a house to address changing needs. In the case of New York State, the result has been a highly inefficient and redundant transportation system.

Anyone with enough common sense to step back for a moment and take in the big picture would see that this is a structure practically handcrafted to impede effectiveness. More often than not, however, people continue to work within structures that were created and that evolved over time with no thought given to how they might affect performance. In New York State, the DOT, Transit Authorities, and MPOs should all be governed at the regional level. A good example of focused governance through an effective structure would be 12 regional transportation boards, each of which includes three divisions: a transit division, an MPO division, and a DOT division. Replacing the existing structure with one like this would result in a more effective transportation network both regionally and statewide, reduce cost, accelerate decision-making and project execution, and streamline governance.

A good example of how this works in practice is the governing structure of transportation units in Nevada. Unlike New York, Nevada had the advantage of developing its oversight of transportation relatively late in life. The state government created two Regional Transportation Districts—Northern and Southern, each with its own board of governors run by elected officials. Under each board, there is a transit division responsible for the public transportation functions within each district, a department of transportation responsible for highways and vehicular traffic management, and a Metropolitan Planning Organization that looks at a region's long-term needs for economic development related to mobility. Placing these functions under a single governing body enables each entity to operate more effectively—a purpose-built house, if you will. Good governance enables good structure, and good structure enables better outcomes. As a result, the cost to manage transportation projects and the time required to execute them are greatly reduced.

Good governance enables good structure, and good structure enables better outcomes.

MATCHING AUTHORITY TO STRUCTURAL RESPONSIBILITY

In structuring any organization, there needs to be parity between authority and responsibility. As a young frontline manager, I was responsible for putting 180 buses into service every morning. This would have been a challenge even with half that number, as it was an old fleet that had not been treated well. The morning pullout was difficult, if not impossible at times. Part of the problem was the limited resources I had been given, but I think the larger problem was my not having the authority to hold people accountable. I had many good employees, but a few underperformers had work habits that were affecting our ability to fulfill our mission every morning. And the solution? Either training to address underperformance associated with "skill," or discipline for underperformance related to "will." Unfortunately, the structure at that time limited any authority I might have had to impose or even recommend discipline, which was disconnected from my responsibility to meet service requirements.

But wait—it gets better: Our Parts division reported to Finance and I was in Operations. Here's why that was a problem: My technicians would routinely run out of the most basic parts required to perform preventive maintenance or repairs but I had no authority to change how parts were ordered or inventoried. This was a structure destined to create conflict. My team's goals were to provide safe, reliable buses to the transportation department (which was my customer); that required, among other things, access to parts. I wanted to maximize availability of parts because I knew the hidden cost of not having parts, including deferred maintenance. (Note: Back then, "deferred maintenance" was the accepted euphemism for "ignored maintenance.") But Finance didn't share my objectives; they weren't concerned about bus availability. Finance was all about minimizing inventory to meet their department's goals. Unfortunately, their minimizing inventory meant I could never maximize availability. Structure does, indeed, have consequences.

Truth be told, I'm a pretty resourceful guy and ended up getting the parts I needed from other buses that were out of service—a process traditionally known as cannibalization. Understanding that "cannibalization" was as bad a term as "ignored maintenance," I replaced it with "controlled substitution," which emphasized my keeping track of whatever parts I removed from one bus to fix another bus. Of course, this was still a rules violation, whatever term you used for it, and, not surprisingly, someone could get fired for cannibalizing a $300,000 bus for a $50 part. But "controlled substitution"—well, it at least sounded like an acceptable rationale for doing something that (let's not forget) really needed to be done.

I needed to meet service, but doing so was not without cost, which leads to another point: Creative, even desperate, management often masks poor structure; as a result, the root cause is never addressed. People end up finding a way to get the job done, no matter what the cost. In my case, the irony was that Finance thought they were saving money by reducing inventory, but the organization was paying dearly by creating double and triple the work. I have this feeling that someone at the top of the agency must have thought that the stripped-down (cannibalized) equipment in every division was just a "communication problem" rather than a structural problem.

> Creative, even desperate, management often masks poor structure . . .

The lesson here: Do not assign tasks without also assigning authority. If you don't give authority to match responsibility at the structural/positional level, don't expect to get the outcomes you were hoping for—it's that simple. Structure and parity have a profound impact on performance.

STRUCTURE AND PURPOSE

In the previous chapter, I spent some time talking about an organization's purpose. One of the key requirements for fulfilling that purpose—and the starting point for all of the other things that go into determining whether an organization will succeed or fail—is structure.

Structure needs to be consistent with purpose. For example, if you're an operating entity and Operations is reporting to Finance, you're confusing your mission and your purpose. Your culture will think and act like a bank.

If you're a sales organization and your external sales team is closest to the customer, everyone in the agency is required to feel subordinate to the needs of the sales manager. The organization must be aligned to help the sales manager sell. Every department—IT, Engineering, Customer Service, Operations, Logistics—must make its objectives consistent with supporting the sales objectives of the agency.

Irrespective of what your mission statement says, your organizational structure will demonstrate to the world how you perform and what you are. It won't matter whether your vision is "to be the most technologically advanced transit system in America." If you have your IT manager reporting to Finance, no one will put much stock in your vision.

Organizational structures are most effective when they are designed to separate the management of uncertainty from the management of commitments. That is to say, execution is most effective on the front lines of an operation when uncertainty (noise) is minimized and commitments are clear.

Every organization needs to know: What is the purpose of what I'm planning to build? What organizational structure will facilitate fulfillment of that purpose? If you know your purpose, then you know what you need now but also what you'll need in the future.

Ideas may bubble up from the bottom, but organizational tone is set from the top. Governance and structure will either confuse or enable clear communication.

So the goal of any organization is to build the structure that will serve its purpose both now and in the future. What happens if you don't have a clear idea of purpose? What organizations usually do is build what they need now and what they think they may need later, and then start fitting in extra pieces later as needs change. It's like building a house—you can anticipate certain needs that you may not yet have (for example, space for children or exercise equipment) and include those rooms in the plans, or you can add on later as each new need arises. The problem with the latter: It isn't always easy to introduce new elements into an existing structure (as was the case with the New York State

Transportation System discussed above). If there's no easy way to build on a wing, you may need to tear down a wall and rebuild part of what's there. And, even if that can be done, it may be impossible to match the addition with the existing architecture or look and feel. Clearly the purpose-built house—the house for which you plan ahead—makes a lot more sense.

Quite often, structure and governance will evolve over years and decades with no one's giving any real thought to the purpose of the organization. A business built to allow for the possibility of expansion consistent with its purpose will be better positioned to take advantage of opportunities than one built to meet present conditions only that has to adjust to future needs haphazardly, with no forethought or purpose.

Industries go through dramatic changes, and those companies positioned to adapt to those changes tend to do better. Think about how computerization changed so many industries. Companies that saw what was on the horizon and built a structure that could integrate computerization did better than companies that didn't have that foresight. Example: A publisher that viewed its purpose as disseminating information would have no trouble getting on board with CDs and DVDs and, later, e-readers. One that saw its purpose only as selling books might face a greater challenge. It's hard to think of a business that wouldn't be wise to factor into its structure the probability of advances in technology in general and automation in particular.

STRUCTURE ENABLES PEOPLE

People work within a structure and are both supported and limited by structure. Put people with the right skills into a structure that supports the purpose of their labor, and you have something good. Put people—even the very best people—into a structure that limits them and works against the purpose of their labor, and you can expect less effective outcomes and perhaps even a failed business.

A transit system needs to work as a single integrated whole. If the signalmen and the conductors aren't communicating with each other, if the conductors aren't communicating with the stationmaster, and if the stationmaster isn't communicating with the webmaster (who publishes the schedule of arrivals and departures), you have chaos. In a business, if Research and Development isn't talking to the product groups, if the product groups aren't talking to Marketing, and if Marketing isn't talking to Sales, you again have chaos. What holds everything together in both cases and accelerates the candid communication critical to organizational effectiveness is structure. But structure can also limit communication. It can enhance culture, but it can also hurt it.

When clear and candid communication doesn't happen, we talk of silos—each department going its own way, people working at cross purposes, nobody talking to anyone else. As you would expect, this lack of good communication has a profound impact on culture. People stop seeing what they do as part of a larger process and lose purpose. More accurately, their purpose begins and ends with what they happen to be doing. Back to my football analogy from Chapter 1: A corporate department that loses sight of the big picture is like an offensive lineman who thinks that all he needs to do is keep his opposite number from getting to the quarterback. The point is, there are other plays in the playbook, perhaps including one that requires him to let the rusher get by him, as in the case of a screen pass. An effective structure doesn't include silos.

People in an organization need to be led. In addition to the underlying infrastructure, structure is about where people are placed on the org chart. Put the wrong people in certain positions—*any* positions—and you have a problem. From the programmer who can't write code to the executive who can't create an atmosphere conducive to motivation and creative thinking, it's a problem. Interestingly, in lawsuits over someone's incompetence, the outcome often depends not on whether that person did something incompetently, but whether the company was negligent in hiring that person—in other words, negligent for inserting someone into a structure or a position designed to fulfill a purpose for which the individual was not the right person.

And just as a well-designed, well-constructed transportation infrastructure enables regional mobility, a well-structured organization enables effective strategy and empowers people. Once the organizational structure is streamlined for parity and optimally aligned with the organization's purpose, an effective organization ensures that it places people in the right positions, identifies talents and gaps in skills, and attends to succession planning.

PEOPLE ALIGNMENT

Performance in an organizational structure is a function of two kinds of alignment. "Structural alignment" enables performance by designing a structure that supports the organization's purpose and ensuring that there is parity between authority and responsibility. "Attribute alignment" optimizes performance by getting the right people into the right positions.

Studies have shown that there are five factors associated with successful job performance in any given position: aptitude, attitude, skills, motivation, and processes. Of these, aptitude counts for about 50 percent. An organization succeeds only if it places its people into positions naturally aligned with their aptitudes.

And aptitude is not a commodity. Think about the natural attributes required for a quarterback, a running back, and an offensive lineman. They're quite different from each other and, at the risk of sharing another understatement, I think we can agree that making an offensive lineman your starting quarterback is not going to win you too many games.

And while I'm at it, here's yet another understatement: People who work in positions that match their aptitudes tend to be happier and more successful in their work.

So how do you get the right people into the right jobs? After trying many different approaches to interviewing, promoting, and hiring new talent, here is a process that I've found to be, by far, the most successful and efficient:

◇ First, résumé screening to ensure that the applicant's background is aligned with the key skill sets and experience required for the position.

◇ Second, an interview to ensure that the applicant is the same person described in the résumé.

◇ And finally, a CPQ (Craft Personality Questionnaire) exam.

For those not familiar with the CPQ exam, here's a quick summary: It takes no more than 20 minutes and determines an applicant's natural attributes, on a scale of zero to 100, in eight basic categories:

1. Goal Orientation—to measure the need to achieve goals quickly, which could be process- or results-driven

2. Need for Control—to measure the need for independence

3. Social Confidence—to measure assertiveness

4. Social Drive—to measure the need to make social connections

5. Detail Orientation—to measure the extent to which decision-making is done through intuition or analysis
6. Good Impression—to measure motivation to leave a good impression
7. Need to Nurture—to measure the need to take care of others
8. Skepticism—to measure trust in others

There are no right or wrong answers on the exam, except within the context of a specific position. For example, an accountant should be all about detail orientation, but an executive who scores extremely high in this category could be in danger of always getting "stuck in the weeds." Put people with high detail orientation in positions where they are making dozens of decisions a day based on imperfect information and watch them struggle. They're not bad people—just in the wrong positions. Or someone with a high "Need to Nurture" score could be exceptionally well suited for many positions involving mentoring or training but could also be exceptionally ineffective in a position requiring productive conflict, which this kind of applicant might naturally avoid. After applicants are ranked for each of the eight attributes, the CPQ process also places them into one of four personality types—Driver, Motivator, Thinker, or Supporter—each of which lines up with certain types of positions.

Following determination of applicant attributes and personality type, the CPQ results are compared with natural attributes associated with success in that position. This extra step of ensuring alignment of personal attributes with position attributes saves time and money in the long run. Think about how much it costs to hire and train employees and then discover that they're not who you thought they were.

I have used CPQ testing for self-awareness, team building, and several other purposes in addition to screening job applicants. Within my existing executive management team, we conducted this assessment and used it to share styles with and among our team. A cohesive team that is aware of its own strengths and weaknesses will be better able to work collectively toward "filling the gaps."

I've also had my children attending college take the test to gain a better understanding of their natural attributes . . . not in a way that inhibits their dreams or vision but in a way that makes them more aware of who they really are and allows them to "fill the attribute gaps" to achieve a desired outcome.

Yes, employees whose natural attributes are not aligned with their position can, in many instances, get by, but only by forcing themselves to compensate for something they aren't. Not surprisingly, they tend to be unhappy at work (and probably in general). They may survive in these positions but will never succeed.

At SEPTA, we had what was known as the "Hawaiian room." It was like the land of misfit toys but was filled with "make-work" positions to accommodate good people who were not well suited to their most recent positions. Rather than terminate them, someone would recommend that they be sent to organizational purgatory (the Hawaiian room) until positions became available in which they could work effectively. As you can imagine, this was bad for both the organization *and* the individuals.

By assessing prospective new hires, you can uncover attribute gaps and more objectively determine proper placement. By assessing existing employees, you can measure attribute gaps and improve self-awareness. If there is a serious gap between personal and job attributes, your employee probably already knows about it. The CPQ process serves to quantify that gap and to present a useful starting point for addressing it.

SUMMARY

✓ Structure both enables and limits performance. Good people will excel in a good structure, but even the best people will struggle to overcome the operational and communications burdens imposed by a poor structure.

✓ Structure must be keyed to the purpose of the organization. Reporting hierarchies that do not reflect an organization's purpose will sabotage internal performance and undermine external messaging.

✓ It's a lot easier to build an expanded structure now than to add on to a structure later. Where specific future needs are still to be determined, smart companies build flexibility into the org chart to allow for rapid and relatively seamless deployment of new functions and reporting relationships, *consistent with the organization's purpose*, that reflect changes in technology or the marketplace.

✓ People work within a structure and must understand the purpose of the structure if the business is to succeed. The right structure accelerates effective communication; the wrong structure inhibits it.

✓ Silos work against purpose and have an adverse impact on culture. People start seeing their jobs as disconnected from the work of other departments and lose sight of the big picture—that is, the organization's purpose.

✓ Structure in a business is about who goes where on the org chart. In addition to ensuring that all parts of the organization communicate with each other and that the right vision and messaging are being communicated to the outside world, a good structure has the right people in the right positions.

✓ A successful structure matches personal attributes with job attributes. The CPQ process is an effective method for getting both job applicants and existing employees into the positions best suited to their aptitudes.

CHAPTER 3

Connections in Transit and Life

Just as making the right connections is essential in transportation for getting to where you're going, identifying and developing successful connections to key stakeholders can often be the critical step in achieving a business or personal objective. The best business relationships exist before a problem arises, and are built on each stakeholder's interests, personality, and communication style.

"**Serving the last mile.**" That's the phrase I often use in referring to the importance of connections in transit systems.

But you don't need me to tell you about the value of good connections in any transportation system. Just think about the last time you took a connecting flight to get to some out-of-the-way destination. I'm guessing that whether you had a positive or negative travel experience was determined in large measure—if not entirely—by how smoothly that change of flights went, rather than the service you received on either flight.

Connections are no less important on the local level. To move people into and out of a city or around a city effectively, transit systems need to develop connections using major destinations and hubs with high-frequency service. Depending on existing infrastructure and the layout of the city, a grid system and hub-and-spoke transit models can work effectively. A bus or rail line must either connect to a major hub or terminal or terminate at a primary location. Missing a bus or train and then having to wait 30 minutes (or longer) until the next one arrives doesn't make for happy commuters. A transit system is only as effective as its connections.

MAKING CONNECTIONS

Connections, along with frequency of contact, are also important in businesses at both the organizational and individual levels. Organizations need to be aware of their major connections, which consist of key stakeholders who help the business achieve its objectives, either now or, more importantly, at some point in the future. As for individuals, they, too, need connections—or key stakeholders—who help them realize their visions, both business and personal. And, much like the connections in a transportation grid, sometimes it's only your second or third connection that provides access to the resource or key decision maker required for accomplishing your stated objective. For example, to develop a relationship with Senator Schumer in New York, I first had to develop a relationship with his legislative assistant Steve Mann. Developing relational equity with Steve was the necessary first step in my gaining the support of Senator Schumer. Just as not every journey by bus or train is nonstop, stakeholder plans often run two or three people deep.

A stakeholder maintenance relationship strategy begins with identification of who is important to you and your agency or department, followed by an honest assessment of the existing relationship, including a review of each stakeholder's interest and influence. For relational status, I would use a 0–5 scale, with "0" indicating that I did not know them or they disliked me (or the organization), and "5" indicating a very close, well-developed relationship. This assessment is followed by an identification of each stakeholder's style to help ensure a positive outcome. In my experience, it's easy to identify current stakeholders who influence the present and help you to achieve stated goals. It's a lot harder to look forward and connect with those who will help you in the future.

Table 2 provides a very general example of the kind of information that needs to be collected and maintained. My actual stakeholder tables were very detailed. They contained personal and business contacts and were continually updated.

Once this preliminary work has been accomplished, it's time for an outreach plan prescribing the frequency and type of contact required to maintain or improve the relational equity with each individual or group. Relational equity is nothing more than the balance in your "bank account" for each stakeholder relationship. If someone knows me because we have talked many times before I ever approach that person for help with a problem, I have some relational equity on which to rely. The account becomes overdrawn when I ask for something without having first laid the groundwork for the request—kind of like asking for a loan from a bank with whom you have no credit experience. Each time you connect with someone *without* making a request or having a problem to address, you are, in effect, making a deposit in that account and (at the risk of overextending this metaphor) demonstrating your creditworthiness.

Table 2. A Sample Stakeholder Table

Department or Position	Stake-holder	Relational Status, 0–5	Personal Style	Relational Strategy and Frequency
Senate	Smith	2	Analytical (bring data and be objective)	Connect funding with local jobs—two in-person visits per year.
Congress	Jones	4	Driver (big picture, avoid detail)	One in-office visit and four phone calls per year. Ask for any open issues. Share updates.
FTA	Dresser	3	Expressive	Two office visits per year. Big Giants fan, enjoys Guinness.
DOT	. . .	. . .	. . .	. . .

The effective use of key stakeholders begins by identifying, for each person, the state of existing relations (good, bad, indifferent) and the interest and level of influence that each person has in your efforts to achieve your goals and your overall success, and then developing an individualized maintenance relationship strategy. This strategy should include, at a minimum, the frequency and type of contact you currently have with each stakeholder, the interests the two of you share, and potential discussion topics.

As director of Maintenance at SEPTA in Philadelphia, I knew I would be called on to fight some major battles with an entrenched and often militant Local 234 of the Transport Workers Union. I also knew that I would need support from transit executives, as well as from other key players in Labor Relations, Law, and Human Resources, in confronting the avalanche of grievances that could be expected to follow any of my attempts to institute significant positive changes in how we did things.

Early in the process, therefore, I identified those key relationships and began building some equity with them. I even reached out to some politicians. When the inevitable grievances were filed and attacks launched against managers, all of these people would know something about me and what the team was attempting to accomplish before they heard a different version from someone else.

I also surrounded myself with managers who had the specific skills and attributes (including very thick skin and rock-solid resolve) required for managing in this type of environment. Bergey, Romano, Davis, Dorety, Crocetti, Gale, Wright, Dooley, Bennett, Hoffmann—each had his own style and set of skills, but all of them had extraordinary intestinal fortitude. And, perhaps more important than any individual attributes, all of us *had equity in each other*. We understood our individual and collective roles and the purpose of our mission, and we protected each other's interests. Connectivity at the human level requires allegiance to a cause, which, in turn, often requires a common enemy. The union leadership in Philadelphia created an enemy that served to accelerate the connections within our team; we had that special kind of equity where you know that everyone else on the team has your back. In circumstances such as these, there's no such thing as too much communication.

> Connectivity at the human level requires allegiance to a cause, which, in turn, often requires a common enemy.

SAVING FOR A RAINY DAY

Identifying potential key supporters for the required changes and developing equity in these relationships meant that when the going got tough, I could count on a loyal group of allies to support my position. As a result, we made significant and difficult changes in a unionized shop that was, to say the least, not predisposed to accept such changes. Penetrating the union's decades-old worldview was helped by including among my key stakeholders union officers and other leaders. Publicly, these individuals had to play hardball with me if they hoped to survive, but behind the scenes they worked toward change. My success in developing and nurturing key contacts was directly responsible for my being able to achieve the change I sought. Without support from my networks—that is, without my equity in connections—it probably wouldn't have happened.

As CEO at CDTA in Albany, New York, my connections had a much more external flavor. Key stakeholders included DOT, FTA (the Federal Transit Administration), members of Congress, senators, members of the state assembly, local mayors, chambers of commerce, economic development agencies—the list goes on. Again, I identified the functions required to achieve our corporate vision; went to work listing people, their interests, and their impacts; and then set about developing relational equity. This consisted largely of spending time with these people so that there would be a preexisting relationship to invoke when I needed their support. I listened before I ever asked for anything. I learned what was important to them and how could I help their interests and the interests of their constituents.

In addition to the standing politicians whom I cultivated as stakeholders, I had to look ahead and find people who would champion my corporate and personal objectives in the future. One such individual was U.S. Senator Kirsten Gillibrand, whom I met at an event in Albany several years before she would run for Congress. I could tell right away that she had a keen interest in transit and mobility. I also had a gut feeling that here was someone who would be in a position of influence in the future, so I added her to my stakeholder list, initially as "low influence, high interest." When, about two years later, she became Congresswoman Gillibrand, winning the 20th District in Upstate New York, I updated her status on my stakeholder list to "moderate influence, high interest." I continued to develop this relationship and, several years after that, she was selected by Governor Patterson to fill the Senate seat vacated by Senator Clinton after she was nominated to be Secretary of State. My stakeholder list was updated again; Kirsten was now "high influence, high interest." Ironically, my daughter and I were having lunch with her at Jack's in Albany when she received the call about the governor's decision to appoint her to the Senate. The point of this story: Stakeholder strategies are like succession plans. They look forward.

> Stakeholder strategies are like succession plans. They look forward.

It's no different than politicians having to develop relationships with constituents. I laugh every October when I receive a flood of campaign literature from local politicians who have been all but invisible up to that point in their term of office. Now, all of a sudden, they want my vote? Maybe some prior contact would have helped. Hey, connections matter. In almost any field, it's a good idea to build them and nurture them.

Every success I've had in my career can be traced to my having identified key stakeholders and building good connections *before* I needed them—to getting in touch with them even when I needed nothing. I would attend community events and volunteer to support matters that were important to them or their constituents. No matter what my own subsequent goal was—whether it was funding for a project or a capital campaign—it was those preexisting relationships that enabled me to achieve it. The lesson here: Don't wait until you need something before you call or visit the people who can help you get it.

NETWORKING TECHNIQUE

The question then becomes: What sort of interaction is called for with these potential allies? Is there one approach that can be used for everyone?

As part of an ongoing exercise for CDTA, I attempted to establish the appropriate type and frequency of engagement to pursue with each stakeholder or group of stakeholders by assessing the potential impact of each according to levels of interest and influence. For this purpose I used a pyramid based on the degree of influence that each stakeholder had on the organization's ability to achieve its objectives, and the current interest that each stakeholder had in CDTA and its mission. The purpose of classifying stakeholders based on interest and influence is to manage time and focus attention on people who influence progress. There are only so many hours in a day. The value of "push" communications (advertisements, email mailing lists, post cards) and "pull" communications (websites, podcasts, video podcasts) cannot be overemphasized. Oftentimes, people move from low influence to high influence and early communications help to accelerate relational equity. Figure 2 displays a sample stakeholder pyramid.

In my current role as managing director of a private-sector manufacturing firm, my approach is no different. I want to know who is interested in my plan and how much this person's or group's influence can bring about the kind of change called for in my plan. My "connections for success" strategy couldn't be simpler: Develop the list, then work to develop equity in key relationships.

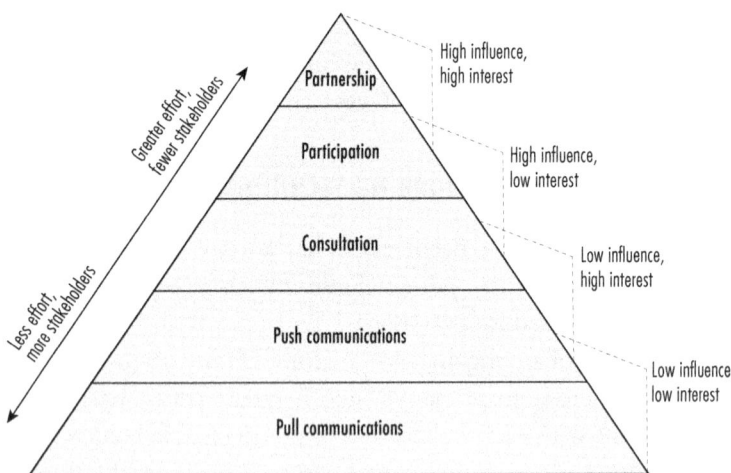

Figure 2. A stakeholder pyramid.

Nothing I've said thus far should be interpreted as a suggestion that you manipulate people. All I *am* suggesting is that you build equity and shared perspective in key relationships (connections), which can be achieved through an honest presentation of facts on the ground, proposed strategy, and potential benefits.

Of course, a little fine-tuning never hurts. Remember: No matter what we do for a living, we're all salespeople. We're always selling something—if not a product or service, then a concept, an approach, a solution, ourselves. When developing a relationship, the most effective salespeople know to adapt to the style of each person with whom they're trying to establish rapport. They align their own style and approach with the interests of their prospects, and tailor their presentation to each prospect's preferred mode of receiving information. To do this effectively obviously requires that they find out all they can about their prospects *before* making a call. Not surprisingly, developing equity in key relationships can be accelerated when you understand who it is that you're trying to befriend.

BEHAVIORAL STYLES

Understanding who you are and whom you're dealing with does not require an advanced degree in psychology. A powerful yet easy-to-use approach to making connections with people quickly and effectively is to classify them as either more or less assertive and according to whether they respond more with logic or with emotion. (See Figure 3.)

I'm going to use myself as an example to illustrate the practical value of this model. The consensus among my colleagues, subordinates, family, and friends—pretty much

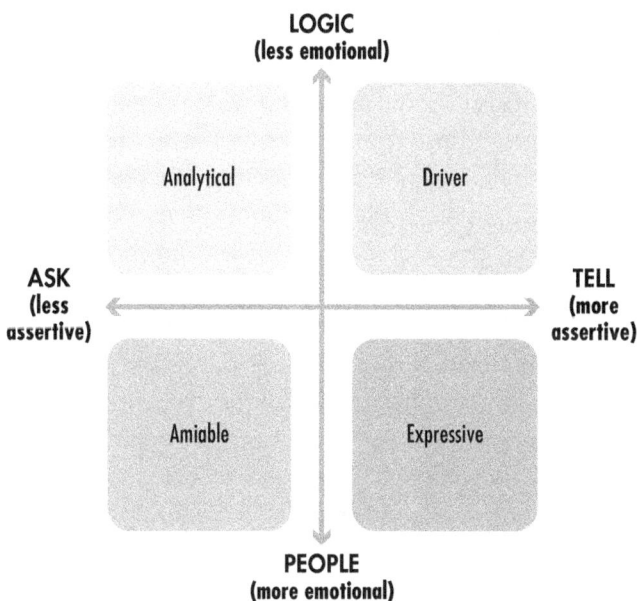

LOGIC
(less emotional)

Analytical   Driver

ASK   **TELL**
(less   ←——————→   **(more**
assertive)   **assertive)**

Amiable   Expressive

PEOPLE
(more emotional)

Figure 3. Classification of people by assertiveness and logic/emotion.

anyone who knows me—is that my personality is naturally more assertive (TELL). I also have lower empathy and am less emotional in business and personal settings (LOGIC). The less-emotional part served me well during my days in Philadelphia, where I was subjected to hundreds of labor hearings and arbitrations and endless hours of cross-examination. Each was a psychologically numbing experience that I might never have gotten through without my "less responsive" demeanor. Not being emotional had the additional effect of really irritating the union and their foot soldiers, who seemed determined to get under my skin and into my head. Being numb to emotion unquestionably helped me at work, although it did challenge me at home.

These behavioral traits—assertive and less responsive—put me on the right side of the chart, probably in the lower section of the "Driver" category but not far from its border with "Expressive." Knowing this, it's clear that I neither need nor want reams of data to develop a thought or a position, but I'm also not quick to agree with an opinion. I want and need streamlined information and expect to engage in a reasonable dialogue before making up my mind. Once I do have an opinion, however, I am decisive. I detest organizations that empanel committees and subcommittees as a way of abdicating their responsibility to make decisions.

(In addition to what I've learned from the results of numerous personality tests, my wife and children have verified my position on this grid with brutal honesty.)

But enough about me. Understanding your key stakeholders and how they behave helps you to accelerate and strengthen the development of key relationships. With any group, seek first to understand and then to be understood. Research your stakeholders' background and preferences; get to know them from a distance. Some information is generally available on social media or corporate websites.

Where it's not, quite often you need to identify behavioral styles through meetings and personal observation.

FORMING A PLAN

Once you've zeroed in on the behavioral styles of your stakeholders, the approach to take with each is logical and straightforward. If an individual is purely "Analytical," I'll bring solid information to the conversation, emphasizing a few key points to develop shared perspective. If they're technical, then I'm technical; if they're social, I'm social. Occupational stereotyping would strongly associate the "Analytical" quadrant with the positions of chief financial officer, engineer, and auditor. These individuals received their education in classroom environments that tended to be devoid of emotion—everything in either black or white, with no shades of gray. Perhaps it's an overstatement (not to mention horribly unfair) to say that any personality these individuals may have had was surgically removed by their sophomore year of college, but I do remember hearing that anyone who made it through college with a four-year degree in finance and still retained a personality was made an economist. But notwithstanding the unfairness and inappropriateness of many of these occupational stereotypes, I think it's safe to say that these individuals are less likely than their colleagues in sales and marketing to want to spend the first five minutes of a meeting talking about last week's football game. They want you to get to the point and support that position with factual data.

On the other hand, it's probably not a great idea to bring a 20-page article to someone in the "Amiable" category. This individual is looking to understand your background and see if there's some level of connection between the two of you . . . and with it, some potential for compromise. With this group, be sure that you understand the other person's position. Because "Amiables" are not naturally expressive, you should plan on using open-ended questions to elicit the information you need for understanding their positions on matters of mutual interest.

In both the public and private sectors, I often interacted with politicians to advocate for investment in transportation infrastructure. The process of funding transportation in the United States is like operating a train at 55 miles per hour while someone is laying track one mile in front of the train; it's hard to see or plan long term.

> Funding transportation in the United States is like operating a train at 55 miles per hour while someone is laying track one mile in front of the train.

As I write this, there are eight committees in the House of Representatives and Senate that oversee different aspects of the legislative process in drafting a transportation bill, all with different and often competing interests and priorities. From an advocacy perspective, I had to be prepared to push the agenda for transit funding to stakeholders with different beliefs, values, and styles. If, for example, the stakeholder happened to be a Conservative Republican (usually, but not always, "Analytical"), I would highlight the increased revenues resulting from a long-term transportation bill, but always within the context of how these increased revenues would create jobs in his or her district. My presentation would always contain hard facts to support the connection between investment in transportation and job creation.

Likewise, if I were meeting with a Democrat (often, but not always, less "Analytical" and more "Expressive"), I would advocate for the same transportation bill but connect the argument to the social benefits of mass transportation, including job creation. But I would also emphasize social equity, access to jobs, air quality, elderly transportation, and many other social and environmental aspects to develop and leverage this stakeholder influence. Understanding the natural behavioral style of a key stakeholder serves to develop equity quickly in a relationship with personal and professional benefits.

When I had completed this analysis of my stakeholders and their styles, I would plug a schedule into my outlook calendar of recurring reminders. The type of outreach could be a letter, a visit, a phone call, or an email, depending on what I had discovered about their communication style and preferred mode of receiving information. Some politicians would prefer to meet me in a bar for a few drinks after work—an opportunity I would never miss. The important thing was to interact regularly with the people who could help me achieve my corporate or personal vision, support a goal, or resolve a problem.

In the next chapter, we'll look at the factors that go into determining how to manage time to ensure adherence to a schedule that is both realistic and responsive to everyone's needs.

SUMMARY

✓ All things are made possible through connections. Make a list of your key stakeholders based on their interest and level of influence in your efforts to reach your goals. Then work the list.

✓ Don't wait until a problem arises before reaching out to your stakeholders. The chances of their understanding and supporting your objectives are greatly increased if you have preexisting equity in the relationship with them.

✓ All of us are salespeople. When building a relationship, do what effective salespeople do: Adapt your approach to each key stakeholder's interests, style, and preferred mode of receiving information.

✓ Interact regularly with your key stakeholders, taking into account as well their behavioral styles (more assertive vs. less assertive, logical vs. emotional).

CHAPTER 4

Staying on Schedule and Time Management

A successful transit system depends on effective time management, which consists primarily of managing schedules during both peaks and downtime. In business, and at a personal level, success is often determined by what we do with our time during both scheduled and unscheduled hours, but especially during our own downtime, when we have more control over how we choose to spend our time.

TRANSPORTATION—it's all about timing.

In Chapter 3, I talked about how important it is for a transit system to provide reliable connections. In fact, the relevance of any transit system depends on its ridership, which in turn is influenced by connectivity, on-time performance, and comparative travel value. Connectivity and timing can make or break a system's effectiveness.

A transit schedule is a commitment—a contract between you and the rider—and the success of a transit system depends on how well it meets that commitment. Do trains and buses arrive when the schedule says they'll arrive? And is the

A transit schedule is a commitment.

schedule based on an empirical logic that reflects the actual needs of riders?

But schedules are only the public (visible) manifestation of that logic. For schedules to meet the needs of riders requires the coordination of myriad moving parts, most of which are never visible to the public. People and purpose are what drive outcomes.

Public transportation is, by its very nature, capital intensive. That is to say, you need a large number of buses and trains to serve the citizenry of any geographically dispersed area that includes a metropolitan center. Having the necessary equipment on hand is simply a matter of making the required capital investment; either you have the budget for what you need or you don't. But whether that equipment gets deployed in a cost-effective manner is a separate issue—one that depends on good time management.

PEAKS AND VALLEYS

In a transit system, time management consists primarily of effectively managing peaks and downtime. A fleet of trains and buses will be used to capacity twice each day and then be used relatively sparingly for hours. How efficiently these assets are deployed and controlled is determined, in large measure, by how well a transit system is able to manage the transition from peak (busy) to off-peak (slow) times.

And it's no different for highways, which are built to manage peak loads. A highway such as I-95 in Baltimore or I-15 in Las Vegas will be crowded at 8:00 a.m. on Monday and near empty at 2:00 a.m. on Wednesday. You don't normally see expressway lanes being blocked for roadwork during rush hour; on those rare occasions when they are, even the most patient and reasonable among us are likely to begin muttering unkind thoughts about state government. Work requiring lane closures is almost always scheduled to be done during off-peak hours (with a few historic exceptions, such as the work done in Fort Lee, NJ, on the approach to the George Washington Bridge, but that's another story). Managing time—including maintaining equipment, roads, and tracks; training employees; and adapting to changing demand—is how a transit system is able to meet the demands of its schedule.

THE BENEFITS OF PLANNING

I started my career in fleet operations and, at a very young age, it became obvious to me that we were being reactive in managing our time. For the most part, we fixed many things when they broke but did little before then to prevent them from breaking. What I learned very quickly is that managing time effectively is possible only when you can plan activities, and that increasing planned maintenance needs to be the primary objective of any maintenance operation. When you plan maintenance, you can control it with standardization, inventory, and timing, among other things. Unplanned maintenance—such as repairing a bus or rail car brought in with an unexpected defect—requires additional resources and undetermined inventory. To the extent that you can plan maintenance, you're able to plan the use of one of your most important and costly resources: human capital.

Life works in much the same way: We all get the same 24 hours each day—no pre-labeled *free time*, *uptime*, or *downtime*. Just plain *time*, and how we choose to use that time is up to us. Do we drive the agenda or does the agenda drive us? Do we make deposits or take withdrawals? Do we improve things or make them worse?

One more point: The ability to optimize time management in fleet operations starts with a well-designed, precisely specified asset. Quite often, buses and rail cars are specified by people who never own the responsibility of maintaining the asset over its useful life. As I noted in Chapter 2, putting Finance in charge of the parts needed for maintenance made it almost impossible for my team to meet its goal of providing safe, reliable buses to the transportation department. That's because Finance wasn't concerned with that objective but rather only with minimizing inventory. When, as here, someone who doesn't own the responsibility for the asset is making decisions about the asset, time management—and especially the effective use of human capital—becomes much more difficult.

WORKING BACKWARDS

So, if time management is the key to operating cost-effectively, and effective planning is the key to time management, it follows that cost-effective operations must begin with planning. That may seem intuitive, but the best approach to planning may not be so obvious. Is this a brainstorming opportunity? A solitary lock-yourself-in-a-room-and-don't-come-out-until-you're-done exercise? An occasion for appointing yet another committee? Is planning a personal matter that depends on the kind of business you're in, as well as a number of other factors that differentiate you from your competitors, or are there general principles that transcend differences among companies and industries? Exactly how *do* we decide what needs to be done to make the best use of our time?

Rather than prescribe a set of steps for the whole world to follow, I'm going to describe what I do. I don't know if this will work for everyone, but I think the underlying principles are at the core of any effective planning strategy.

First, I look a year into the future and work backward. What are my top five goals for the year and how are they connected to my long-term vision?

Having planned my year, I now plan my month. What will I focus on this month to move me closer to my annual goals?

I then plan my week. What do I need to focus on this week to make my month productive?

Finally, I plan my day. What one or two things will I work on today to address issues of importance proactively? Today, for example, I will choose to spend 30 minutes exercising, to spend time with my children, to make the tough calls and hold the tough interviews (such as for discipline or termination), to say something nice to someone I love, to write a personal letter or card (*not* an email) to someone important, to conduct evaluations, to walk around and speak to employees serving on the front lines, and so forth.

My schedule is often preloaded with travel, presentations, and client meetings. In between those scheduled events, however, I have the opportunity to choose how I spend my time. Those precious openings present choices that will often determine how successful or healthy I am in business and in life.

Choose to use your unscheduled time to do what's important. For me, that includes exercise, reading a book, writing notes to clients, calling a family member, and getting organized.

And here is the irony of choice management: When you take the time and make the choice to engage in proactive, high-value activities, you reduce the amount of time spent simply reacting to less important activities and dealing with emergencies (which are, by definition, unplanned). Either you drive your schedule or your schedule drives you. Yes, something I learned in bus maintenance at 19 years of age still applies every bit as much in my life today.

In equipment maintenance, it's what you do with equipment off peak that determines how that equipment will perform during peak demand. Investments made off peak pay dividends during peak periods. Life is like that, too.

While I was Director of Maintenance in Philadelphia, it was not unusual for my union section officer to file dozens of grievances in a single day in an effort to distract managers from their agendas. Choosing to address those grievances without neglecting our planned activities was critical in changing how business was done within our operations. It took some effort and a good deal of situational awareness to prevent this or any union section officer from setting our agenda with frivolous grievances. Forgive me for inserting yet another sports analogy here, but think about a football team that has its defense on the field for most of the game. No matter how well the defense plays, that team is probably not going to win the game unless they can get their offense out there to score some points. (Yes, technically they may shut out their opponent and win on an interception or blocked punt, but how often does that happen?) Or, stated otherwise, you're very unlikely to succeed, on the field or in business or in any aspect of your life, by letting someone else set the agenda. Make sure your offense gets on the field.

CHOICE MANAGEMENT

In a general sense, time management is really choice management. It's about what we choose to do with ourselves (or our assets) with the time available to us each day. We cannot

Time management equals choice management.

manufacture additional hours; everyone gets 24 in a day. All we can do is choose how to use or not use those hours. Time management equals choice management; in the case of my own experience with fleet maintenance, choice management was not an option without planned maintenance.

In business, unplanned and unstructured time has a way of taking control of your day. Every minute you're not actively engaged in some productive activity of your choosing is likely to generate two minutes of time you'll have to spend on some activity not of your choosing. Time management is the sine qua non for everything you do. You need to manage your time to ensure that you get product to market on time, disseminate communications about product in time, and reply to customer inquiries or concerns in time. As with a transit system's need to accommodate both peak and off-peak loads, you also need to balance the urgent with the less critical in such a way that you aren't constantly putting out fires but rather working to prevent them.

In spite of its absolutely essential place in the running of a transit system or the running of a business, time management continues to crop up on everyone's list of "Things I wish I could do better." I think that may be because the key to managing your time is to "know thyself," and not many people take the time to do that. I mean, sure, we all have a general sense of what we're good at (such as "well organized," "big-picture person," and "a closer") and what we're not so good at (such as "can't add," "long-winded," and "unable to delegate"). What we don't always do, however, is act in a way that plays to our strengths and accommodates our weaknesses.

Successful managers take stock of exactly what they're good at and then surround themselves with people who can handle all of their other tasks much more efficiently than they can. They also have *perceptive awareness*—that is, an understanding of how they think and what biases they have that may be acting as filters for how they see and interact with their environment. One of my early managers and mentors at SEPTA was Luther Diggs, who was a master at self-awareness. Luther was keenly aware of what he liked and didn't like, and who he was and was not, and he surrounded himself with a team that compensated for and complemented his weaknesses.

As with transit systems, any business will have its uptimes and downtimes. Although we think of those uptimes as the "important" times—the times when things get done and we need to be at peak performance—it's actually the downtimes that can have the more important long-term impact on our business or personal lives. The uptimes we can't control, but it's those other times where we get to exercise our discretion in deciding how we spend those hours which can determine how successful we are. Do we watch TV? Read a book? Spend time with family? Or do we just wait to react to life or someone else's agenda?

EMOTIONS TAKE (AWAY) TIME

I want to conclude this chapter by noting the role that emotions sometimes can play in our efforts to manage time and by providing an illustration of how moving beyond emotions is often the key to maintaining the focus required for dealing with difficult challenges. Many—probably most—people tend to hold a grudge when wronged by a coworker or anyone in a personal relationship. Yet hatred is a huge drain on our emotions and our time. Choosing to hate or to spend time even thinking about hate is a bad choice. Managing time requires managing emotions; if you hate or return the hate you receive from another, you waste hours that will never come back to you.

A personal friend of mine, Jesse Broussard, was the first African American bus operator in Houston following the passage of the Civil Rights Act of 1964. Prior to the passage of this legislation, Broussard worked for the Metro but was permitted to do only janitorial work, as black employees were not yet allowed to drive buses. On his first day as an operator, he showed up in uniform. So happy for his new opportunity, he arrived an hour before start time and boarded the bus to wait for his instructor. At five a.m., his instructor walked onto the bus and said to him, "Get off my bus, n____. I will never train you to drive." Understandably upset, Broussard waited in the drivers' room all day, then returned the next day to hear the same racist rant from his would-be instructor and others. Undeterred, he returned the next day and the days after that until eventually he received the training and certification he required to operate a bus. Despite the cruelty shown to him, Broussard never lost focus. He never made any attempt to get even with those who had verbally attacked him, even when he was promoted to head of operations for Metro and was supervising many of the same employees who had treated him so inhumanely during his training. Some asked for forgiveness and were told by Broussard, "I forgave you many years ago." He made a choice not to let others control his agenda. In making that choice, he avoided wasting emotional energy and time on people who probably would have preferred that he react differently.

The weak never forgive. Forgiveness is an attribute of the strong.

SUMMARY

✓ Managing time effectively requires planning. Unplanned maintenance, for example, will require additional resources, undetermined inventory, and excess human capital.

✓ When making decisions about an asset rests with someone who doesn't have responsibility for that asset, time management and the effective use of human capital become much more difficult.

✓ Time management is choice management. We cannot manufacture additional hours, only choose how we spend the hours available to us.

✓ Successful managers determine or already know their strengths and weaknesses and surround themselves with people who can provide support in their areas of weakness.

✓ Successful managers also have *perceptive awareness*— that is, knowing what biases may be coloring their relationship with their environment.

✓ What we do during downtimes, rather than times of peak activity, can have the more important long-term impact on our business or personal lives because it's then that we have more control over how we spend our hours.

✓ Managing time requires managing emotions. When you let your emotions determine how you act, you lose both focus and time that can never be retrieved.

CHAPTER 5

Developing the Strategy

Strategic planning provides a road map for getting companies or individuals from where they are today to where they would like to be in the future. It is used to map the course from vision to reality through a multi-step process that works backward from the vision to general goals and specific objectives. To be realistic, however, strategic planning must begin by considering your present position and resources.

WHAT IS STRATEGIC PLANNING?

STRATEGY IS HOW we materialize vision. Strategic planning is a dialogue with key stakeholders about vision and vulnerability for sorting out what we can and can't influence and identifying what we want to achieve and need to avoid. Strategy, in its early stages, is more about questions than answers. It's more about problem identification than problem solution. There is nothing worse than a solution in search of a problem. Strategy is as much about creating a "not to do" list as it is identifying what to do. Strategy is about identifying patterns. Peter Senge said that the human mind is conditioned to see life as a series of events. If this is true (and I believe it is), strategy is about stepping away from the event to see the larger pattern. Finally, strategy is about drawing a distinction between cause and symptom so that the organization can focus on root-cause solutions to identified weaknesses.

Throughout this book, I've talked quite a bit about the importance of planning. In this chapter, we're going to take a deeper look at strategic planning, which, in one form or another, can be found on the to-do list of just about every successful business entity.

In a nutshell, we need strategic planning because the future never gets here, and yesterday ended last night. Done correctly, strategic planning creates deliberate movement between the present and a future desired state—it is essential for the organization. It allows us to capitalize on the past, rethink the present, and embrace the future. From a business perspective, strategic planning represents an attempt to seek strategic advantage through the full utilization of human resources. Later, we'll see how it can provide important benefits in one's personal life as well.

A strategic plan is a road map for future operations—how to get from Point A to Point B—but it also creates a shared perspective of what we do and why. Whether in a transit system, in business, or in your personal life, it identifies where you'll be at some point in the future in relation to where you are today, and outlines a plan to close the gap between the two.

In the absence of strategic planning, the corporate default is what I like to call the Heritage Strategy, which basically requires that you restrict activities and thinking to what has made you successful in the past. Is there a better example of this than Washington, DC? Would it be naïve of me to speculate that nothing new ever gets accomplished there because what gets taken seriously is pretty much limited to what has already been established as "safe ground"? Congress can barely get together on *old* ideas; I wouldn't hold my breath waiting for a bold new national vision any-time soon. A variation of this found in many companies is the "not invented here" syndrome. A vision or part of a vision that takes decision makers out of their comfort zone stands little chance in these companies of becoming the basis for a refreshingly new vision. Virginia Postrel does a good job of highlighting this battle between forward- and backward-looking visions in her book *The Future and Its Enemies: The Growing Conflict Over Creativity, Enterprise, and Progress*. She sees a parallel between the argumentative and divisive nature of American politics and the tension be-tween those who would like to live in a world that doesn't change and those who see change as part of life.

In fact, history is littered with examples of individuals and companies that have looked back to (re)create their dated visions. But the future will never confuse memory with vision even if our minds allow it to. All of this isn't to say that you ignore what has made you strong, but that you be aware of changing circumstances and adapt to new realities. Your loyal workforce and cus-tomer base is counting on you.

> The future will never confuse memory with vision even if our minds allow it to.

Be careful as well that your vision and your plan are attached to a purpose. In general, people do not respond to a strategic plan; they respond to a purpose. They want and need to be involved with a greater reality. The most effec-tive strategic planning explores and communicates purpose first and plans afterward.

PLANNING IN TRANSIT

Most of my education in strategic planning came from working in transit systems. The basic truth there, as in busi-ness, is that it's not enough to react quickly—you need to anticipate the environment and the circumstances in which you'll be acting. Admittedly, it can be extremely difficult at times to step out of today's reality to see tomorrow's possibility, but leadership requires no less. Specifically, you must look both inside and out to gain an understanding of what you can influence and what you can't. Knowing what you're powerless to influence tells you what you'll need to avoid. If this sounds a lot like the first stanza of Reinhold Niebuhr's "Serenity Prayer,"* be aware that the wisdom contained therein is no less important in a business context.

From a business perspective, strategy taught me to engage stakeholders. It taught me to identify problems and to ask questions. By engaging in a discussion of vision and vulnerability, we separate what we can influence from what we cannot, and what we want to achieve from what we want to avoid. In the process of engagement, shared perspective (buy-in) is created. As an outcome, and a collateral benefit, creative minds are attracted to an organization with a progressive growth strategy of which they'd like to feel a sense of ownership.

Some writers have said that culture will eat strategy for breakfast. I believe this is incorrect. Managers live within culture, and leaders understand and shape culture for the benefit of the organization. This requires an element of inclusive strategic planning. Culture governs people's actions, and those actions eventually come to define the culture. The culture of any organization is shaped by the worst behavior that its leadership is willing to tolerate, and by the

*God, give me grace to accept with serenity
the things that cannot be changed,
Courage to change the things
which should be changed,
and the Wisdom to distinguish
the one from the other.

best behavior that it is willing to recognize and reward. Strong culture includes candor, introspection, and shared perspective, all of which involve strategic planning.

> The culture of any organization is shaped by the worst behavior that its leadership is willing to tolerate, and by the best behavior that it is willing to recognize and reward.

Transit systems are a great place to learn the importance of strategic planning because the consequences of both good and bad planning are as clear and dramatic as anywhere. In a typical business entity, you may be dealing with the impact of a good or bad quarter on long-term growth and market share. In a transit system, on the other hand, you're dealing with whether an entire fleet of buses or commuter trains can meet revised safety standards and technologically or economically updated rider expectations. The consequences of poor planning can be more transparent—sometimes painfully so.

On May 12, 2015, an Amtrak Northeast Regional train from Washington, DC, bound for New York City, derailed and crashed on the Northeast Corridor in the Port Richmond neighborhood of Philadelphia (which is, by the way, very close to where I was born and raised). Of 238 passengers and five crew on board, eight were killed and over 200 injured, 11 critically. When it derailed, the train was traveling at 102 miles per hour (164 kilometers per hour) in a 50-miles-per-hour (80-kilometers-per-hour) zone of curved tracks. The sad reality is that the technology to prevent this accident had been available for two decades prior to this incident.

Beginning in 1990 the National Transportation Safety Board (NTSB) included Positive Train Control (PTC) on its Most Wanted List of Transportation Safety Improvements. (PTC is able to automate such functions as collision avoidance and speed enforcement.) At the time, the vast majority of rail lines relied on human crews for complying with all safety rules, and a significant fraction of accidents were attributable to human error, as evidenced in several years of official reports from the Federal Railroad Administration (FRA).

In September 2008, Congress considered a new rail safety law that set a deadline of December 15, 2015, for implementation of PTC technology across most of the U.S. rail network. The bill, ushered through the legislative process by the Senate Commerce Committee and the House Transportation and Infrastructure Committee, was developed in response to the collision of a Metrolink passenger train and a Union Pacific freight train in California on September 12, 2008, which resulted in 25 deaths and injuries to more than 135 passengers. The bill never included a dedicated funding source and the projects were never implemented in a timely manner. As of this writing, rail systems across the country have failed to implement decades-old technology that is both proven and effective at protecting capital and saving lives.

What was needed: problem identification followed by problem solution. Effective strategy would likely have identified this problem and this technology long before legislation. It would have identified the opportunity to improve safety and protect capital. It would have identified the threats posed by avoiding its implementation and it would have identified improvements required to fixed infrastructure and rolling stock and their respective costs. The gap between what existed in 1995 and what was required would have been part of an annual review. Year after year, the gap in funding would have been highlighted, resulting in coordinated marketing and advocacy strategies. I am not saying this would have resulted in completion in the '90s, but certainly, in my view, effective planning and advocacy would have led to implementation long before that tragic event of May 2015.

An element of strategy includes deliverables for accomplishment. A strategic plan without resources, or a plan to acquire needed resources, is nothing more than a dream.

At the Berridge Facility in Philadelphia and as CEO in Albany, New York, I worked with key stakeholders who developed, wrote, and signed off on strategies to create ownership. This resulted in accelerated improvements wherein all key parties understood why things were being done and what impact they would have. It also created an accelerated acceptance of the inevitable. Strategic planning gets everyone pulling in one streamlined direction. It accelerates change and improves everyone's understanding of how individual roles are connected to collective outcomes.

In 2004 when I was first hired as COO in Albany, NY, the state's Public Transportation Safety Board (PTSB) was ready to take over maintenance operations after years of reported safety violations. Bus fires, brake failures and wheels falling off were unfortunately routine. Absent a written plan with acceptance and buy-in, our team would never have been able to turn around operations in short order. A crisis is a terrible thing to waste.

A crisis is a terrible thing to waste.

For my first year in this position, the PTSB had me report improvements to it on a regular basis until its members felt confident that programs were in place to maintain assets in a continued state of good repair. The *Albany Times Union* would routinely run stories about how poorly maintained the transit fleet in the Capital Region was—stories that were painfully accurate. Improvements that would have typically taken years in a public sector unionized environment were accomplished within months. The people involved understood why and bought into the process. As a result, accelerated change occurred. Needless to say, strategic planning is important in business and in life. So what makes up a good strategic plan?

Perhaps the best way to understand what makes for a successful strategic plan is to recognize first why strategic plans fail. Organizations spend hundreds of millions of dollars each year on strategy, and too often well-written, meaningful plans sit on bookshelves in executive offices collecting dust. There are reasons they don't live out their envisioned outcomes. Here are the top six:

1. Lack of stakeholder buy-in
2. Unclear goals
3. Improper organizational structure
4. Absence of purpose
5. Lack of accountability
6. Inadequate communication/feedback loops

That's what doesn't work. So what does work? There are four steps in any effective strategic plan (see Figure 4):

1. Groundwork
   a. Stakeholder identification and engagement (Chapter 3)
   b. Prepare the mind
   c. Create the Vision (Chapter 1)
   d. Examine organizational structure (Chapter 2)

2. Inputs
   a. PEST assessment
   b. SWOT analysis

3. Analysis
   a. Risk
   b. Value and cost

Groundwork		
Prepare the Mind	Identify and Engage Stakeholders	Create the Vision

↓

Inputs	
PEST	SWOT

↓

Analysis	
Risk	Value and Cost

↓

Outputs
Actionable Plan with Resource Allocation and Implementation

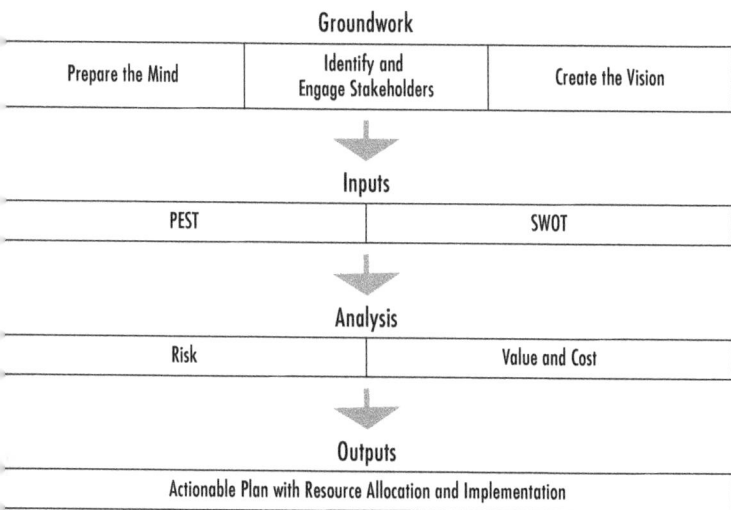

Figure 4. The four steps in an effective strategic plan

4. Outputs
   a. Written plan
   b. Implementation tables
   c. Accountability structures
   d. Commitment page

Let's consider some of the key components in each of these steps.

STEP 1—GROUNDWORK

PREPARE THE MIND

I've touched on the importance of identifying and engaging key stakeholders in developing a strategic plan. In short, you need to hear from people with different perspectives and unique experience. In addition, when developing a strategic plan it's wise to examine beforehand how we think about the future—to prime the mind, if you will. This is important because, when thinking about the future, our minds persist in trying to trip us up and our eyes see only what the mind is prepared to comprehend.

Table 3 offers a quick look at the default structure of the human mind. When the mind is stimulated by an event or thought, we process this through our unique filters and examine our unique files to determine an action or response. This happens instantly and automatically, with no analysis or examination on our part. For the unprepared mind, the default usage is to prove others wrong and ourselves right. Our minds are hardwired; the older we get, the more difficult it becomes to squeeze a new thought through circuits burned by time and events. In the unexamined mind, yesterday will often hold tomorrow hostage.

> In the unexamined mind, yesterday will often hold tomorrow hostage.

Strategy requires a deeper level of thought. In preparing to think about the future, we need to recognize our deeply held beliefs and understand that they can create a bias that

Table 3. The Default Structure of the Human Mind

Personal Content Filter	Personal Filing Cabinet
Confirmation biased by emotional tags	Unusual X-reference
Small percentage of data—by default we are driven more by emotion than logic	Past-based and limited
How will this impact me?	Perceptions and opinions (converted to facts over time)

Default Content Retrieval	Default Purpose
Instant	To protect ourselves
Automatic	To prove ourselves right
Unexamined	To prove others wrong

often prohibits new ideas and directions. Think about what goes through your mind as you prepare to consider strategies for the future. In the early stages of strategy, problem identification and questions are more important than answers. Ask a lot of questions and listen with an open mind.

CREATE THE VISION

As noted in Chapter 1, a good place to start thinking about strategy is with the purposes of strategic planning. One of those purposes is to create a vision of the future and determine what is needed—*today*—to materialize that vision. In other words, we're working backward—from future vision to present circumstances. (Note: Vision aligned with purpose is an especially beautiful thing, and purpose aligned with passion is magic.) Strategy also serves to identify strengths and weaknesses with brutal honesty; identify challenges and opportunities; align strengths with opportunities; to the extent possible, develop objectives that mitigate weaknesses and challenges (threats); and identify external political, economic, social, and technological changes that can either help or hinder your progress.

Once these determinations have been made (and even the most detailed analysis comes with no warranty), you're ready to create your organization "playbook." This will contain an approximate course of action that includes resource allocation, candid self-awareness (which includes being open to an external assessment of who you are), setting priorities, and creating competitive advantage.

If you have never done strategic planning, don't worry about it. You still won't find much of it in Washington or, for that matter, in most state and local entities. We live in a great nation but one that lacks a cohesive strategy for mobility and education at the national level. Generally, this failure can be attributed to most elected officials' being focused more on reelection than on transformational leadership. Perhaps nothing would do more to help get this country going in the right direction than having term limits for elected officials. Imagine if the better part of a two-year Congressional term were spent on solving problems, rather than on getting reelected. But I digress.

So imagine instead a nation with a 20-year plan for investment in mobility and infrastructure—a plan that includes insulated revenues and dedicated resources for implementation and oversight. A plan such as this would require a champion and a process for winning acceptance—a process that would, itself, become part of the strategy. Once such a plan is accepted, you can create the circumstances that attract creative capital, both intellectual and financial (in the form of private-sector dollars). More than a few officeholders and candidates for higher office have talked about the difference between reacting to circumstances and actually shaping the future. Developing and implementing a strategic plan illustrates as well as anything what they're describing.

You can create the circumstances that attract creative capital, both intellectual and financial.

Most programs at the state or federal level in this country are debated and funded on an annual basis, which is, again, like operating a train at 55 miles per hour while someone is laying down tracks one mile in front of you. What's often missing is vision, which is an ideal starting point in developing your strategy playbook. If you don't know what you want your business or your personal life to look like in five years, take a few minutes to think about it. People who have a vision—even if they have nothing else—have a huge advantage over people

People who have a vision . . . have a huge advantage over people with no vision.

with no vision. It's not easy working toward a goal if you don't have a goal, and not easy finding a goal worth working toward if you don't first have a vision.

Nonetheless, strategic planning often starts with "what is" and seldom with "what could be." Does this contradict what I just said about starting with a vision? Well, not really. You begin with a vision and thereby, at least temporarily, separate yourself from current reality. Once it's established, however, you also need that vision to be viewed *in the context* of your current reality. The identified actions taken monthly, quarterly, and annually are designed to close the gap between where you are and where you want to be. Without the proper resources, a vision will remain just that—a vision.

In getting us from Point A (where we are today) to Point B (where we'd like to be in the future), a good strategic plan considers the likely future outcomes of present actions. What we hope will happen can never be the sole foundation on which to build a strategic plan, but neither is what has already happened. *Hope is not strategy, and history is not destiny.*

Caveat: Just as my saying back in Chapter 1 that you ought to dream big and then do what's necessary to get there wasn't intended to suggest that you "live in vision" all the time, so my statement here that "hope is not a strategy" is not intended to suggest that you "live in circumstance" all the time. Dreaming big is not only important but necessary if you're going to achieve long-term success in a dynamic marketplace. How realistic your time horizon is, however, does depend on where you are today and how well you (at the individual level) or your team (at the organizational level) can execute the identified actions required to close the gap. Your five-year strategic plan shouldn't take 10 years to get off the ground. I'll have more to say about execution—and the frequent divergence of execution from even the most carefully designed strategic plan—later in this chapter and in the next chapter.

STEP 2—INPUTS

PEST

Businesses often do a PEST assessment as part of the strategic planning process. In my business, this involves annually reviewing the external environment for changes to several areas. A template for an assessment from a transportation perspective might look like this:

- ◈ Political
  - Regulatory changes—emissions, seat belts on buses
  - Increased privatization
  - Homeland security funding
  - Immigration policies
- ◈ Economic
  - Federal & state funding
  - Labor costs
  - National economy, inflation
  - Gas prices
- ◈ Social
  - Use of social media
  - Terrorism & impact on public spaces
  - Increased trend to share capital—car-share or Uber
  - The biking culture, population growth rates, aging population
- ◈ Technological
  - Applications for mobility that use transit data
  - Electrification of drive propulsion systems

- Increased frequency of cyber attacks
- New or increased focus on surveillance
- Predictive analytics
- Telematics
- Neurolytics/real-time video training

Analysis of these factors would feed directly into the strategic plan. For example, a transit system in Texas or California will need to consider what impact immigration policies will have on its ability to hire and retain frontline staff, including how these policies could affect labor rates. At SEPTA, strategic planning helped everyone stay the course when things became difficult during the militant, 40-day work stoppage in 1998. We anticipated pushback and developed strategies to act (or not act) depending on what was occurring and what, if any, patterns were visible. We were strategic, not controlling. We managed complexity with preparation and training.

> We were strategic, not controlling. We managed complexity with preparation and training.

SWOT

The key to developing timely goals and objectives, as well as successfully executing the tasks that appear in your strategic plan, is understanding the internal strengths and weaknesses with which you'll be confronting the external opportunities and threats that stand between you and your completed objectives. For this purpose, businesses often undertake a SWOT analysis.

A typical SWOT table in transit will look something like Table 4. Each objective requires a strategy keyed to the quadrant in which you find yourself and/or your company.

Table 4. A Typical SWOT Table for the Transit Industry

Strengths	Weaknesses	Opportunities	Challenges
Teamwork	Communication	Leadership	Age of workforce
People	Vision	Planning	Training
Deadline focused	Buy-in from union	Training— regional	Funding—no long-term view
Safety focused	Organization	Administrative support	Contractors
Motivation	Expertise	Utilization of data	All-electric vehicle
Culture of accountability	Labor shortage	Preventive maintenance improvement	Competition for resources
Adaptive workforce	Training	Outside services to generate revenue	Aging population
Commitment	Union leadership	Union relations	

◇ Strength + Opportunity → Strategy to maximize opportunity
◇ Strength + Threat → Strategy to minimize threat
◇ Weakness + Opportunity → Strategy to minimize weakness by taking advantage of opportunity
◇ Weakness + Threat → Strategy to minimize weakness and avoid threat

In all aspects, it's important to align strengths with opportunities, and mitigate weaknesses and threats by determining how we can lessen their impact on our agenda. A word of caution: Be careful not to treat symptoms. Ask questions and identify true root causes. Hint: Weak communication is generally a symptom. Dig deeper.

A SWOT analysis can be applied effectively to a transit system, a business, a department, or your personal life.

An individual SWOT can be the foundation of a candid examination of your strengths, weaknesses, opportunities, and threats or challenges. In Chapter 3 I talked about stakeholder relevance and engagement, which is an analysis that grows directly out of this stage of the strategic planning process.

STEP 3—ANALYSIS

At the conclusion of the input exercise, you will have a list of strategies that need to be examined and prioritized based on risk tolerance and value to the organization. This list could be lengthy and there needs to be a basis on which to focus and streamline action. The risk analysis is based on impact to the organization and likelihood of occurrence. Figure 5 shows an example of acceptable versus unacceptable risk, and every agency will be different.

In 2004, during my startup at CDTA, thermal events (bus fires) were a major issue for our organization. This was identified during our first conversation on weaknesses,

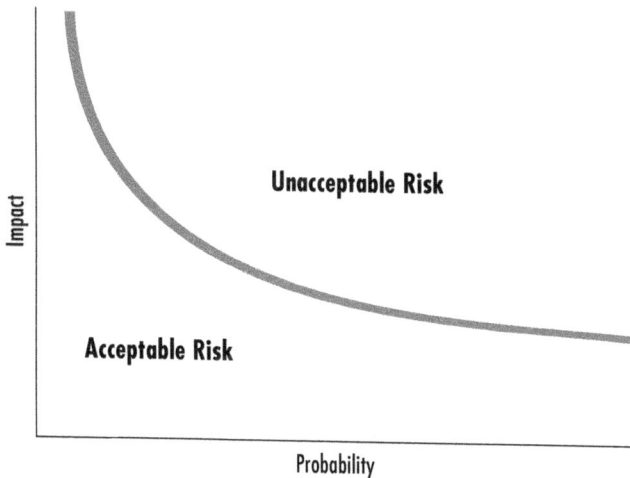

Figure 5. A risk tolerance curve—acceptable versus unacceptable risk.

and a quick examination of risk placed this at the top of the impact scale; within the then-current reality, a thermal event was moderately probable. This positioned this weakness well above our risk tolerance level, so we developed and prioritized several strategies to mitigate (short-term) and eliminate (long-term) bus fires at CDTA.

RISK TOLERANCE

Once you funnel all of your strategic ideas through risk analysis, you can use a value/cost tradeoff table to select and prioritize the most important initiatives based on value to the organization and cost in time or money. (See Figure 6.) Identified items that are rated high value/low cost

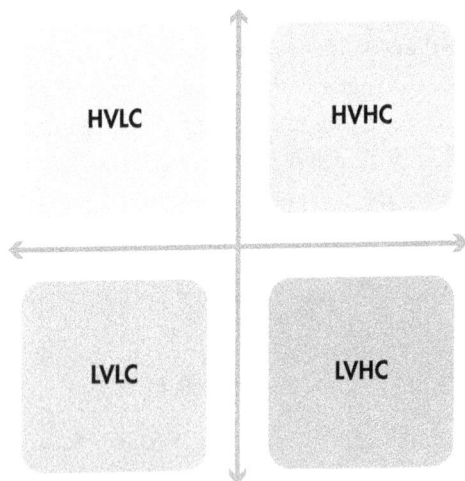

HVLC   High value to the organization and low cost in time or money—this is low-hanging fruit and should be a priority for implementation.

HVHC   High value to the organization with high cost in time or money (a longer-term objective with a longer return on investment).

LVLC   Low value to the organization with minimal cost—this may make the list of objectives but will not be a priority.

LVHC   Initiatives in this category are generally classified as distractions and noise.

Figure 6. A value/cost tradeoff table.

("HVLC") would be considered low-hanging fruit and placed high on the list of goals for the agency. These would be followed by high-value/high-cost ("HVHC") items, which would include longer-term objectives, and finally a review of low-value ("LVLC" and "LVHC") initiatives. In consulting, I often encounter maintenance management teams that identify the following weaknesses: manpower shortages, accountability, training, parts availability, and absenteeism. In analyzing these through the value/cost model, it's obvious that training, accountability, and parts availability would be addressed long before manpower is added. Manpower could be a weakness but is likely a symptom of the higher-value/lower-cost initiatives related to training and accountability. Absenteeism is also likely a symptom of the absence of accountability. A value/cost analysis helps you to separate and prioritize key initiatives.

STEP 4—OUTPUTS

You have prepared your mind, identified and engaged key stakeholders, examined organizational structure, and listed and analyzed inputs, all of which bring you to the output phase. This phase includes a documented action plan with organizational goals, objectives with implementation tables, accountability structures, and commitment signatures.

GOALS

One of the primary outputs prior to determining your objectives will require developing, organizationally or personally, three to seven goals. Examples in a transit environment might include "Grow revenue," "Improve efficiency," "Improve access to information," "Grow ridership," and "Improve the customer experience." Your goals will then be broken down into objectives, which provide the specific action steps required to achieve each of these goals.

OBJECTIVES

Once you have articulated your vision, performed PEST and SWOT analyses, and developed your goals, you're ready to define your objectives—you know, those pesky little things you'll need to achieve if your vision is ever going to become something real. For example, if your vision is to be the market leader in your field, then you'll need to fill in the blanks on such questions as what market share is required, what types of employees you'll need, how much of an R&D investment will be required, and the amount and type of advertising called for. Strategic planning means working backward, from broad vision to narrower objectives to detailed personnel and logistical specs. It requires individual objectives that are aligned with departmental objectives and organizational objectives, all of which are in alignment with vision. I would always reduce objectives to an implementation table, which is nothing more than a systematic way to identify each objective with a target completion date and an owner.

When your analysis is complete and your objectives have been articulated, you're ready to draw up your strategic plan, which, at this point, consists of a list of tasks required for meeting objectives, as well as key milestones and metrics for gauging success. It should also include accountability structures, which I'll talk about in Chapter 7.

EXECUTION, REVIEW, AND UPDATE

Having gone through the steps just described, it's now time to execute your plan. One of the more challenging aspects of working a strategic plan is moving from planning to execution. To do justice to the subject would require a chapter of its own, which is what I've provided with Chapter 6. There we look at this challenge in depth, including descriptions of how several real-life companies spent lots of time in planning sessions but still executed poorly from an operational perspective.

Following execution, you'll need to review and update your strategic plan. *Strategic planning is dynamic, not static.* When circumstances change (and they always do), you'll need to update your strategy and aligned objectives.

STRATEGIC PLANNING
ON A PERSONAL LEVEL

Strategic planning is also important for the individual. On a personal level, it is an attempt to align your natural attributes with your efforts to maximize your potential in life. In fact, some of the issues that can be rather complex when considered in an organizational context—for example, what the potential return on a particular opportunity is and what level of risk it justifies, as well as whether something (such as a blip in the housing market) is a trend representing a genuine opportunity or just a temporary aberration—can be remarkably transparent when applied to one's personal life. For example, will going back to school for an advanced degree make a large enough difference in annual income and the benefits accruing therefrom to justify the time away from family? The raw data that go into the left side of that equation are readily available, and the correct answer for the right side depends entirely on your own feelings (and presumably those of your family). It doesn't depend on any mysterious external factors, as it would when considering, for example, the future price point of a particular piece of

Successful people make a practice of writing down their goals. technology. Successful people make a practice of writing down their goals. You can think of that as simply Step One in personal strategic planning, the next step of which will be, as in the case of organizational planning, to translate those goals into a series of individual tasks.

Of course, not everything in life is planned; spontaneity always seems to find its way into the action. And, although it may sound counterintuitive, I think spontaneity is too important to leave to chance. Because of my interest in thoughtful planning, my annual goals include:

1. To enjoy life more fully.
2. To spend more quality time with family and friends.
3. To pay greater attention to health and wellbeing.
4. To continually learn and develop new skills and knowledge.
5. To make better use of my time (choice management).
6. To organize my efforts and leverage time with technology.

These goals become the basis for some very specific and actionable objectives.

SUMMARY

✓ A strategic plan is a road map for getting businesses and individuals from where they are today to where they would like to be in the future.

✓ Strategic planning accelerates change by helping all parties understand the reasons and potential impacts of actions taken, thereby putting everyone on the same page toward a shared purpose.

✓ Strategic planning generates an organization "playbook" that contains an approximate course of action that includes resource allocation, self-awareness, setting priorities, and creating competitive advantage.

✓ Strategic planning begins with an individual or organizational vision, but a vision that takes into account current position and resources. Otherwise, it will never become more than a vision.

✓ As part of the strategic planning process, a PEST assessment involves periodic review of the external environment for political, economic, social, and technological changes, all of which could require modification of the strategic plan.

✓ A SWOT analysis provides an understanding of the external opportunities and threats that stand between you and your completed objectives, as well as the internal strengths and weaknesses with which you'll be confronting them.

✓ A good strategic plan is no guarantee of success. Much depends on execution, and the ability to make the difficult transition from planning to execution.

✓ Strategic planning is a dynamic process. Following execution, the plan must be reviewed and its objectives updated to reflect changing circumstances.

✓ On a personal level, strategic planning can be used to align your natural attributes with efforts to maximize your potential.

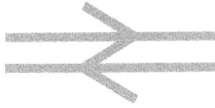

CHAPTER 6

Getting It Done

Effectively executing a strategic plan requires vision, operational know-how, and the emotional intelligence required to connect the organization with a future outcome. Communication with stakeholders and employees is essential to bringing a plan to life, as is someone in authority to champion the plan. You also need to be sufficiently flexible to modify the plan as it bumps up against reality.

"No battle plan survives contact with the enemy." We've all heard that in one form or another. The full quotation—by Helmuth von Moltke the Elder, a Prussian general—is closer to: "The tactical result of an engagement forms the base for new strategic decisions because victory or defeat in a battle changes the situation to such a degree that no human acumen is able to see beyond the first battle." In these or any of its paraphrased forms, the point is the same: You can plan all you want, but the moment you try to execute your plan, you'll probably find that you need to be adaptive if you're going to have any chance of succeeding.

Profound? Sure. Catchy? You bet (the short version anyway). Yet the suggestion is hardly surprising. You develop a plan pretty much in a vacuum—in an isolated room with a bunch of people far removed from the action. Plans are about as theoretical as it gets. Yes, all of the planners have experience. They have access to data, both historical and current, as well as to market and industry forecasts. They may also have access to outside expertise. What they don't have is a means for testing their plan under real-life battle conditions. Simulations may shed light on certain aspects of the plan, but they're still only simulations that, given marketplace instability (some would say entropy), may bear no resemblance to what will actually happen when you try to execute your plan. Is it any wonder that most strategic plans fail to deliver on their objectives?

RULE #1: NO STRATEGY EXECUTES ITSELF

In early 2006, I was appointed to the New York State Senate High Speed Rail Task Force. The purpose of this task force was straightforward—to identify barriers and recommend strategies that would enable high-speed rail (HSR) to operate on the Empire Corridor between Albany and Penn Station in New York City. The Empire Corridor was the fourth-busiest corridor in the country and was terribly underserved.

As discussed in Chapter 5, it's always a good idea to begin the strategy formulation process by defining your vision. As a task force, we agreed that by 2025 we wanted to establish a New York State rail corridor of national significance and international recognition that would achieve the following:

◇ Link all major metropolitan areas
◇ Provide the next generation with reliable, frequent, and affordable public transportation
◇ Be environmentally responsible and sustainable

- Encourage the development of intermodal transfer centers
- Foster economic and sustained growth

The task force also wanted to identify all prior studies related to HSR that might have preceded our project.

In fact, we found 23 previous feasibility studies on HSR related to this corridor. The earliest was a 1970 study and action plan that looked at cost and feasibility for HSR in New York State and this corridor specifically. I don't know what the cost was for HSR in 1970 but I do know that, 46 years later, not much has changed in New York State HSR except for the cost of implementation, which has grown exponentially. Avoidance comes at a cost.

Avoidance comes at a cost.

To recap: 23 studies and action plans over a span of 40 years and nothing to show for it. A passenger-train trip from Albany to Penn Station takes roughly the same time today as it did in 1970. The lesson to be learned from this: Resources expended on planning don't always have a connection to an outcome.

Resources expended on planning don't always have a connection to an outcome.

Some of the older studies we looked at outlined Maglev propulsion, a technology initiated in New York State but later deployed and perfected by rail systems in Europe and Japan. *Through the use of magnets, a train is able to move without being in physical contact with the track, thereby reducing friction to allow significantly increased speeds. (Maglev = Magnetic levitation.)* The first prototype Maglev train was demonstrated in New York State in 1913. That's more than 100 years ago.

Study after study shows the need for improved HSR options between Albany and New York City. In spite of that, nobody has taken any action, but we are again making the case. I never like being part of something that may never get put into action.

WHAT I LEARNED

Through my involvement in the New York State High Speed Rail Task Force, I became aware of several barriers to making HSR a reality. First, service on the corridor was unreliable. The track between Albany and New York City was used both for freight trains, which operated by the calendar, and for passenger trains, which operated by the clock. In addition, the track was owned in portions by three different entities: AMTRAK, Metro North, and CSX.

Segregation of interests and investments will always be a challenge with multiple owners. The main barrier to implementing HSR was unity of control. Along with other members of the task force, I felt that we needed to focus attention on gaining unity of control of the right of way and the tracks for several reasons.

- ◇ Ownership and operations were fragmented throughout the corridor.
- ◇ Freight traffic was increasing.
- ◇ A single owner (a state authority in this case) would facilitate the investment in right of way and administration of betterment fees (when track structure materials are replaced with improved materials).

We did our due diligence. We provided justification for HSR on this corridor and developed strategies for track asset valuation. We also put together a very focused implementation plan that was recommended to the Senate in June of 2008. The plan, however, lacked a champion—someone who would provide authority and resources—and that needed to be someone political. At the time that I became part of the twenty-fourth plan to put HSR in New York State, the state was in political turmoil due to the controversy surrounding Governor Spitzer's indiscretions.

We were never able to find the champion that we needed, and a great plan absent a champion is just another piece of paper. I'm sure that at some point in the future, someone will commission another task force that will find 24 documents to establish the background for planned improvements. For the cost of 24 studies and plans, we could have purchased that right of way!

> A great plan absent a champion is just another piece of paper.

In every business organization, a good leader is both a strategist and an implementation champion. On a personal level, you are the champion of your own plan. But in an organization, you'd better make sure that the champion of your plan is someone with appropriate authority. All strategic plans require executive sponsorship to be effective.

In fact, there are strategic plans all over the world, both personal and business-oriented, that do nothing but lie on shelves and collect dust. In fact, I'd guess that for every 10 or 20 people able to think about or create a strategic plan, there may be only one person capable of making a plan a reality. From a hiring standpoint, companies need to understand that the attributes needed in a planning position are different from those required in the person who will be executing the plan.

> For every 10 or 20 people able to think about or create a strategic plan, there may be only one person capable of making a plan a reality.

ACCELERATION ATTRIBUTES

Beyond just hiring the right people, you need to enlist everyone in your organization in the effort to execute your strategic plan, which requires that *you instill in them* the attributes needed for effective execution. Here are a few that I believe can accelerate the execution of strategic plans in a business organization:

- ◇ Purpose—As already noted in another context, people respond to purpose, not to plans. Purpose is what connects everyone in the organization to a reason to sign up and work toward a common outcome. Successfully linking a strategic plan to a purpose is what generates buy-in and accelerates execution.

- ◇ Delegation—Effective execution and effective delegation are pretty much synonymous. If you develop a plan with input from key stakeholders and then try to micromanage its contents, your efforts to execute that plan effectively are going nowhere. Micromanagement of a strategic plan is a sure recipe for failure.

- ◇ Absorbing noise and giving credit—In the process of executing plans, leaders run interference against "the machine"; this is especially true in larger organizations that manufacture lots of red tape. Leaders also take every opportunity to give credit to others for their contributions to progress. As leader, your role is often to separate the bureaucrats from the people who are productive.

  > In the process of executing plans, leaders run interference against "the machine"

- ◇ Finding an enemy—No, that's not a misprint. Allegiance requires a cause, and a cause requires an enemy. At the Berridge facility, despite our attempts at inclusion, the union opted to attack the management team and set up a roadblock to anything that had even a hint of progress about it. In hindsight, their attack contributed sig-

  > Find an enemy.

nificantly to unity among management. It's no exaggeration to say that having an enemy facilitated our success.

◆ Intestinal fortitude (i.e., guts)—In business, it takes courage, determination, and (yes) endurance to see the implementation of any plan in the face of the many obstacles and barriers that may confront it. Obstacles may arise in the form of people, politics, and resources. He or she who owns the execution responsibility must see it through, not with stubborn tenacity (which is not the same thing as the three attributes mentioned a couple of sentences earlier), but with adaptive intelligence. If my operations team needed new technology to do their jobs and someone in procurement refused to approve the purchase order, I would write the justification. If it was still denied, I would call that technology something else, give it a different part number, and reorder it. There's no need to bang your head against a wall when there's a way around the wall.

◆ Social and emotional intelligence—This means knowing yourself and how to leverage the collective network of people around you to achieve an outcome. Emotional intelligence enables the mind to suspend judgment with a keen sense of self-awareness.

◆ Sense of team—In executing a strategic plan, a leader evaluates people not so much on the basis of their individual skills but rather on their ability to operate as a team—to protect and help each other. I have worked with many smart people—lots of PhDs and MBAs—including some with extraordinarily talented technical minds who were not good team players. I never cared for brilliant loners. They are not desired, and certainly not needed, in an environment that requires collective effort. Technical skills pale in importance compared to the psychological and moral qualities of a good team member.

◇ Awareness—Being close to field intelligence and knowing what's happening on the playing field are keys to implementing a plan in business. In any execution phase, you're going to have a range of players that we can conveniently (and alliteratively) label "Family," "Friends," "Fence-sitters," "Fighters," and "Foes." Each of them has a distinct role to play, requiring a different leadership style for you to engage or eliminate, summarized in Figure 7 on page 96.

During the process of execution, people within categories will change. Foes will become either Fighters or Fence-sitters, and Friends will become either Family or Fence-sitters. By the end of the process, you will likely have about 60% Fence-sitters, 20% Fighters, and 20% Family. Your job as a leader is to know where the players are at any given time and to "move the chains." My own experience suggests that success depends on the ability to move people through effective communication.

KEYS TO SUCCESS

So much for your people, but what about you? What attributes are required of a leader charged with bringing to life a strategic plan? We know that creating an effective strategy isn't easy. It requires vision, and vision requires unfiltered imagination that connects people to purpose with a sense of enthusiasm. But, as I hope I've impressed on you by this point, executing a strategy is even more of a challenge. It requires the operational know-how to convert that vision into reality with concrete action steps and firm accountabil-

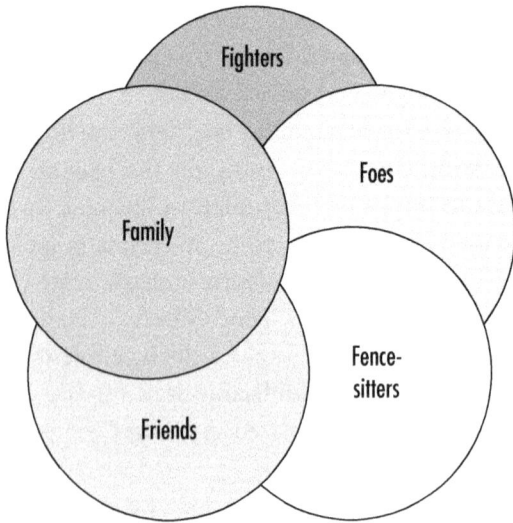

Fighters	Foes	Fence-sitters	Friends	Family
Committed to making change fail	No reason to be involved in making change work	Waiting to be persuaded that changes are good	See changes as important but not essential	Committed to making change really work
Opposed	Opposed	Neutral	Want change to succeed	True believers
Active opposition	Passive opposition	Looking for signs	Passive supporters	Active supporters
Silent saboteurs or noisy, open, and confrontational	Fear of significant increase in workload	Waiting to check management's stomach for change	Want to see management and change advance	Acceptance of need for change; true believers

Position	Strategy
Fighters	Ask them what they need to support the change.
Family	Engage them as change agents and champions.
Fence-sitters	Keep them informed and build their involvement.

Figure 7. The range of players.

ity structures. It requires personal drive and interpersonal skills that communicate and foster commitment.

To put that in a slightly more human context, it takes people with vision to create great strategic plans; it takes people who can understand and communicate with people to execute those plans successfully. If the formulation of a strategic plan means closing yourself away in that isolated room with other people and synthesizing data and ideas from multiple sources, then the execution of a plan means opening those doors and engaging multiple constituencies whose support you will need in the execution phase.

I think there are several keys to success in strategy execution, most of which involve a turning outward from the intensely inward-focused development phase. I say "most of which" because there is really no discrete point at which you "turn outward" with stakeholders—you need to be engaged with them during every stage of development, and to obtain their signoff once the plan is completed. Beyond that, however, you need to connect the dots—that is, ensure that all employees connect what they do with the outcome of the strategy. As noted in Chapter 5, your strategy cascades from vision to goals to departmental and personal objectives. Your chances of successfully executing the plan increase significantly if you sequence your objectives and break tasks into prioritized steps.

It goes without saying (but I'll say it anyway) that good communication is essential. Monitor and coach your people. Let them know for which deliverables they will be held accountable. Measure the plan's progress and, of course, recognize and reward employees and departments that are contributing significantly to it. Realize as well that a strategy is always an approximate course of action. Be prepared to adapt as your plan bumps up against reality. As a leader, commit to creating a compelling image of the future and then "walk the walk" to improve your organization . . . and yourself.

That's a lot of directives for one paragraph. Let's take a moment to unpack some of it.

As is so often the case in business and in life, the key to succeeding with a strategic plan is to start from the endpoint and work backward. Begin by envisioning what things will look like with your plan fully executed and then determine what's needed to get to that point. Perhaps the most obvious requirement: You're going to need buy-in from your team, and to get people on board you'll need to make sure they know where the finish line is and what first prize consists of. You need to get your employees to own the content, and that's not easy to accomplish without first letting them in on where things are headed.

Communicating with your employees—not just a progress report every couple of weeks, but an ongoing bidirectional dialogue—is critical. You need to be present and accessible. Staying close to your employees also helps in identifying barriers and building in strategies to work around or through them.

I talked in a previous chapter about the importance of deadlines in creating and increasing your employees' investment in a project. Perhaps nowhere is establishing this level of accountability as critical as in the execution of a strategic plan. Develop implementation schedules and attach a timeline and an employee name to each. An implementation schedule is a sequenced list of events, with each event having a name and a date associated with it. If the plan spans several departments or divisions within the organization, identify deliverables for each. To motivate employees to embrace assigned requirements, set up accountability structures that specify both positive and negative consequences. Then, as the plan is being executed, tie everything together with a review process that reinforces the positive and negative consequences of adhering or not adhering to the implementation schedule. There is nothing worse than having a plan with assigned responsibilities and no accountability. The reality is that people will do almost anything to remain firmly ensconced in their comfort zones; to secure their cooperation with the tasks and timetables associated with plan execution, leadership requires that you coax people out of those comfort zones.

In chess, they say that having a bad plan is better than having no plan. Truth be told, I'm really not crazy about either option in a business organization, but at least having *some* plan—even one that may not address the full gamut of challenges and opportunities awaiting the organization—will still tend to energize everyone around a shared purpose . . . *provided that the organization acts on that plan*. A plan is better than no plan, but a plan that sits idly on the shelf is probably worse than no plan.

TEAM COMMITMENT, INDIVIDUAL ACCOUNTABILITY

At the Berridge facility in Philadelphia, we faced extensive institutional resistance to the steps outlined in our strategic plan. In 1998, coming fresh off a 40-day strike characterized by tremendous labor unrest, we developed and distributed a plan designed to close the gap between where we were and where we wanted to be. Executive leadership at SEPTA wanted immediate and lasting change at the Berridge facility. My timeline was months, not years. It seemed to me that many employees took this plan about as seriously as they had taken all of the plans that preceded it—as just another set of empty words destined to be an important-looking desk ornament/dust collector. The difference this time, however, was that we included implementation steps that had names and dates attached to them. *People were going to be held accountable.* More important, they *understood* that they would be held accountable. In the heat of battle at Berridge, we hung a large banner from the ceiling in one of our production departments. It read, "People who say that it can't be done should not interrupt those in the process of doing it." We wanted the employees being pressured by the "protectors of the past" to understand that we supported them. We communicated the message verbally, on signs, and by taking action. People were held to account. Not surprisingly, we succeeded in executing the plan in an environment that many would consider irremediable.

> People who say that it can't be done should not interrupt those in the process of doing it.

During the execution phase of a plan, the executive who champions the plan must balance focused advocacy with open-minded inquiry. That is to say, you need to advocate for the plan and its outcomes while remaining open to outside critiques and adapting to changing realities. At Berridge, I was responsible for the plan and was also its champion. I surrounded myself with a tremendous team of managers, each with different strengths and weaknesses that complemented those of the others. As a group, we were the complete package. I had soldiers, generals, techies, and enforcers, all with their own unique roles. I purposefully found people who would compensate for my own weaknesses. The plan had many other champions, each of whom was referenced within the document. To ensure my people's commitment to successful execution of the plan, every included strategy

> Balance focused advocacy with open-minded inquiry.

> We were the complete package—soldiers, generals, techies, and enforcers, all with their own unique roles.

had an implementation table associated with it, and every implementation step had a date and name attached to it. Whenever a significant strategic plan was finalized, I required every one of my direct reports to sign the last page and commit to the execution of its contents. There was no room left for doubt in anyone's mind—they were an integral part of the plan. Collectively we could "move the chains"; individually we would fail.

A good manager never assumes a static environment. Take another look at Figure 7. Each label provides a convenient way of describing an employee, but no label is guaranteed to be permanent. This is especially true of Fence-sitters. By just sitting back and letting nature take its course, you are effectively empowering those who oppose you to convert those Fence-sitters into Fighters and Foes. By confronting the enemy head on, however, you can neutralize their position and indirectly convert the Fence-sitters into Friends and Family. In this kind of environment, confronting bullies is a sure way to convert nonbelievers. Go after the loudest, largest obstacles to your plan and let them know—publicly, if the opportunity arises—that either they're in or they're out.

> Let them know—either they're in or they're out.

Just such an opportunity presented itself to me once during a toolbox meeting with about 40 technicians and front-line management. When a discussion of how we planned to implement standards on the shop floor became heated, I reminded one of the ring leaders who was working hard to preserve the past that our mission was one of public service. "This is our mission and this is our purpose," I told him before a packed house. "You can either accept and support it or get out and find one you *can* support." We were able to convert a few Fence-sitters at that meeting, and he was never that vocal again.

"FIRE IN THE HOLE"

The standard catcall on the shop floor—"fire in the hole"—was used to warn other employees of impending management presence and to try to intimidate me or other managers. Hearing "fire in the hole" had the same effect on me as my high school English teacher's telling me that I would never amount to anything. Rather than intimidating me, it only served to motivate me. "Fire in the hole" was that person's way of saying that he wanted special attention. I would hear it and immediately walk over to whoever said it and spend time with him, talking and smiling. This was very difficult for people on the floor at this time because anyone spending more than a few seconds with management would often be accused of being a rat or a narc. Other managers did the same—we would not be stopped. As described above, at Berridge we planned, and then we enjoyed progress. That's because the message got out quickly enough: Management is playing for keeps, and there will be consequences for anyone who doesn't get on board with the plan and its execution.

I had a similar experience in Albany, where there was a huge gap between the kind of transit agency we were and the kind we needed to become. Our strategic plan developed shared perspective and brought accountability to the process, resulting in significant progress. I would be lying if I said that every employee jumped on board with the execution of our strategic plan, but the majority certainly did. As an organization, we began to pull in one streamlined direction. When that happens, progress is inevitable.

SUMMARY

✓ A strategic plan has value to an organization only if it is executed.

✓ A strategic plan is theoretical—most fail to deliver on their objectives because they are created in a vacuum.

✓ Resources expended in planning don't always have a connection to an outcome.

✓ Successful execution of a strategic plan requires having someone to champion the plan—someone with the appropriate authority.

✓ The attributes needed in someone in a planning position are not the same as those required in someone responsible for executing the plan.

✓ It is the responsibility of the leader to instill in every team member the attributes required for effective execution.

✓ As intensely inward-focused as plan creation may be, plan execution needs to be outwardly focused. Communication with stakeholders and employees is critical.

✓ A strategy is always an approximate course of action. Be prepared to adapt in real time.

✓ Motivate employees by giving them a sense of how they will be contributing to the plan, and by holding them accountable for making those contributions. Play for keeps!

CHAPTER 7

Accountability in Business and Life

In transit systems, as in all business entities,
success begins with accountability. Whether
positive (in the form of praise) or negative (in
the form of consequences for failing to do
what was required), accountability contributes
most effectively to a successful outcome when
individual requirements are communicated
beforehand and contextualized as part of an
overall team effort.

GOOD TRANSIT SYSTEMS—bus and rail systems that run
on time and provide safe and comfortable travel to their riders—require strong levels of accountability to support their
performance. The relationship between accountability and
system performance is fundamental: Accountability drives
personal performance, and personal performance drives system performance.

In 1992 I was a frontline manager at SEPTA's Callow-
hill Division in Southwest Philadelphia. I worked from
11:30 at night until 8:00 the next morning. The manager
running the organization was a very compassionate person who believed that (1) people should be given unlimited
chances to perform, and (2) compassion trumped account-

ability. I, on the other hand, expected people to come to work and perform their duties to the best of their ability.

Those who didn't perform needed to be trained or held accountable. It was either skill or will, can't or won't.

The fact is, most did but some didn't. I believed that those who didn't perform needed to be trained or held accountable. It was either skill or will, can't or won't.

Even as a young man without benefit of higher education, I knew that without accountability the good would eventually go bad and performance would decline to the lowest common denominator. I didn't agree with my manager and, unfortunately, was too young and too stupid to appreciate that at times you need to do what's popular if you want to be around long enough to do what's right. I required people to be on time and work to a standard, and I backed

At times you need to do what's popular if you want to be around long enough to do what's right.

that up with discipline, only to have that discipline overturned within this "culture of compassion." Bad employees were protected, the performance of good employees predictably sank in the absence of consequences, and service suffered. As an organization, we showed compassion to all employees, but at the expense of our mission and ridership.

What, exactly, is compassionate management? I think of it as a "harmony-over-truth" management style that tolerates poor performance and bad behavior. When a compassionate management philosophy is used to guide an organization, people are encouraged to present themselves as sufferers and victims, not as self-reliant employees. Under this administration, SEPTA was loaded with victims who would voluntarily come to work each day only to complain about how bad work was. Although discipline was frowned upon, I still felt compelled to ask some of our worst victims why they even bothered to endure the pain of another week. Why not just stay home?

Fortunately for me, when I returned to SEPTA a few years later, it was as part of a turnaround team under executive leadership that supported and expected workforce accountability. It took several years of very difficult change management to overcome the damage done by the culture of victimization created by compassionate management. In spite of the many good employees at SEPTA, it was, with few exceptions, the victims and sufferers who had set the pace. And management was squarely to blame.

SETTING STANDARDS —
ONLY THE BEGINNING

Accountability is at the root of a transit system's ability to succeed. If the schedule is unreliable, if riders are not enjoying a safe and comfortable ride, if standards across the board are not being met—someone needs to be held accountable. The only thing worse than setting standards and not having them met is setting standards and *not caring* whether or not they are met. In other words, having standards but no accountability.

I've talked in previous chapters about what goes into a good transit system. We need to meet rider expectations, and we need a way of measuring how well we're meeting those expectations. But we also need accountability, not simply to lay blame on someone for failure to meet expectations, but, of even greater importance, to determine who is responsible for fixing the problem and how the problem can be avoided in the future.

With any accident or failure to deliver on-time performance, it's obviously important to determine the cause, and not just for legal reasons. The administration of accountability will always start with questions, including:

The administration of accountability will always start with questions.

◇ Was the standard operating procedure clearly communicated?
◇ Were the employees properly trained on the work process or standard?
◇ Were there special circumstances to consider in this instance?
◇ Was the exception intentional or accidental in nature?

Perhaps the speed limit needs to be reduced on a certain stretch of track. Or perhaps a bus itinerary needs to be changed to avoid a heavily congested or high-accident area. System performance goals become far more achievable when drivers, engineers, maintenance and administrative workers—all employees—understand the consequences of their failure to follow standard operating procedures, rules, and guidelines and its impact on the customer.

In the maintenance environment, standards set the baseline for accountability. Without standards, performance tracking and reporting are irrelevant. When I became director of SEPTA's Berridge Facility in 1997, employees were taking between 70 and 80 hours to rebuild a 6V-92 Detroit Diesel Engine. An Allison B400 Transmission required somewhere between 40 and 50 hours. Removing a powertrain from a bus would take close to a week. This level of performance was ridiculous on its face, but the absence of standards meant that there could be no accountability and, without accountability, people worked down to the performance of the slowest individual or team. Absent work standards, the lowest common denominator sets the pace.

Absent work standards, the lowest common denominator sets the pace.

We invited union leadership to talk about the problem. They ignored our invitation. So we evaluated the job process (including times) in real time as the work was being completed and then set and communicated work standards. We also notified the workforce that it would be expected to meet these standards and would be held accountable.

Once standards were set, a few people had to be written up and/or disqualified for not meeting them. But lo and behold, suddenly performance times fell dramatically. Rebuilding a 6V-92 dropped from 70 hours to 36–38 hours, rebuilding that same Allison B400 was now taking 16 hours instead of 40–50 hours, and removal of the powertrain from a bus no longer took a week but only about five hours. These order-of-magnitude differences in performance could be attributed simply to our setting standards and administering consequences. By the way, "consequences" included recognition for progress, not just discipline or demotion for nonconformance.

Many would assume that a transformation of this type and magnitude would be extremely difficult to accomplish in a militantly unionized environment. Well, I'm here to tell it *was* difficult, but the management team enjoyed it because we were responsible for "moving the chains" and making things a whole lot better than they'd been for a long time.

ACCOUNTABILITY AND PEER PRESSURE

Human behavior doesn't happen in a vacuum. When behaviors shift and mutate in a group setting, they generally do so in reference to how other people are behaving. That's because people will naturally do what they can to avoid pain. In some work settings, pain can take the form of being harassed by one's peers for working faster than they do, and the way to avoid that pain is to conform to the norms of the group, namely, to work slower. The way for management to short-circuit this pattern is to substitute a more powerful motivator than peer pressure. If workers see their peers being held accountable for lackadaisical performance, their counterintuitive need to work slower to avoid harassment will be replaced by an intuitive need to work to a reasonable standard.

As a young helper, I was called a "job killer" for changing tires too quickly. My manager never said "nice job," and my peers never stopped giving me a hard time. With no positive or negative feedback from my manager, and with no standards or accountability, what was I supposed to do? Somehow I survived, which is all I wanted to do in that environment: Survive long enough to be in a position to succeed and change things for the better.

ADMINISTERING ACCOUNTABILITY

Accountability is not some complex, highly abstract concept. It is management that sets standards for performance by communicating the level of performance that is expected, then monitoring performance, and then holding people accountable. And it is management that determines how quickly accountability will become part of the culture and how much "teeth" it will have when administered.

With regard to the administering of accountability, a leader has three basic options: positive feedback, negative feedback, and no feedback. Incredibly, most managers choose no feedback, then move on to negative feedback if that doesn't work. Effective leadership understands that accountability includes a combination of positive recognition and, where required, negative consequences. Accountability is a support network for successful people.

Accountability is a support network for successful people.

This is no different than what happens in one's own personal or professional life. Every year I set goals, write them down, share them with a manager or friend or mentor, and then measure my performance against those goals. My personal goals can be categorized as mental, physical, social, and spiritual. After I've signed on to them, I go to work on achieving them. I hold myself accountable. The absence of accountability has real-life consequences. We see some of them every night on the news and read about them the following morning in the newspaper. Ninety percent of leadership (and life) is about follow-up—measuring what was expected and being candid about progress or regression.

FINE TUNING FOR INDIVIDUAL SUCCESS

Outstanding managers always remember that each of their direct reports is unique and that their chief responsibility is to arrange roles, responsibilities, and expectations that can best draw on, leverage, and help further develop each employee's unique contributions. Accountability sometimes has unintended consequences in that employees often will find themselves in positions that are not well aligned with their skill sets. Setting standards and holding individuals accountable may require removing people from their assignments and placing them in different assignments—ones in which they can succeed. Within my accountability "caseload," I always derived the greatest satisfaction from those instances in which employees were disqualified for not meeting a standard and then placed in a different position in which they ultimately succeeded.

Accountability and discipline should not be used as an escalator to termination. Rather than placing an employee "on a program" (i.e., on probation)

Accountability and discipline should not be used as an escalator to termination.

as the legally required prelude to termination, managers should use accountability and discipline as tools for modifying substandard performance or objectionable behavior. For employees who were unable to meet a standard, I always tried to determine: Was it skill or was it will? If a lack of skill, I trained first, then reevaluated. If a lack of will, I administered progressive discipline—for example, a written warning, followed by a one-day suspension, a three-day suspension, a five-day suspension, and then a final warning—to offer as many opportunities as possible to get the employee back on track. In many cases, I would demote a person to a lesser role before termination. The reality is that a good technician is hard to find. When you do find good people, you need to be sure that they're trained and placed correctly.

Success in life is about making sure that your skill set and natural attributes are lined up with your occupation. If you select carefully, you'll love what you do and it will never really feel like work. And remember: Expecting high performance is a prerequisite to its achievement. High standards and optimistic thinking will not guarantee a favorable outcome, but their absence will most assuredly create the opposite. Accountability must follow expectations.

ACCOUNTABILITY AS MOTIVATOR

Whether in a transit system or a corporation, the process is the same: Accountability drives performance, and performance drives success. Accountability is nothing short of a competitive advantage. Even in our personal lives, the extent to which we succeed generally reflects the extent to which we choose to hold ourselves accountable.

I'm not opposed to compassion as a human attribute—only as a management strategy. As noted previously, when you let compassion take precedence over accountability, you encourage your people to present themselves as victims and sufferers and not as self-reliant human beings.

When you let compassion take precedence over accountability, you encourage your people to present themselves as victims and sufferers.

On the other hand, *passionate* management develops, trains, and involves people. It holds them accountable for what is expected in work and in life. Holding people accountable for their performance is not cruel; its benefits accrue both to the individuals held accountable and to the people who depend on them to perform at a high level at work and in life.

THE DARK SIDE OF GROUP PROCESS

In business, there is a tendency to solve problems by committee. Hey, I like a good brainstorming session as much as the next guy, and, when it comes to solving complex problems requiring multidisciplinary expertise, having four or five heads (assuming they're the right heads for the task) figures to be a much better strategy than relying on just one person to work everything out. From a strictly PR standpoint, committees also serve to give the impression that one is bringing to bear maximum firepower to deal with the problem.

But let's not forget that there's a price to be paid. Committee members are often able to hide behind the dispersed responsibility of a committee, making it more difficult to identify the party responsible for addressing specific aspects of the problem. As a result, some committee members may feel less than totally invested in finding a solution to the problem. The bottom line on group problem solving: Less is often more.

How much less? If you ask me, nothing energizes an employee like being asked to fly solo, and nothing de-energizes an employee like being an anonymous contributor in a group setting. Try this experiment sometime: Ask five employees to work as a group to produce a single report. Then ask five other employees to work as a group to submit individual reports. I'm pretty sure that—controlling for individual employee knowledge and skill—the separate reports will show evidence of much greater care in their preparation than will the single group report.

The funny thing about accountability is that while all employees require it, good employees actually desire it. I believe that people want to be involved, trusted, and held accountable. This is no different from

> People want to be involved, trusted, and held accountable.

being held accountable at a personal level. Being accountable means that *you matter*. Everyone—at least at a personal level—wants to matter.

Accountability really comes down to a choice: Are we victims and sufferers, or are we self-reliant human beings who want, despite everyday obstacles, to move our agenda forward?

POSITIVE ACCOUNTABILITY

Many employees hear the word "accountability" and immediately equate it with "blame." But accountability also has a positive side. It's also about identifying those people who are primarily responsible when things go right.

It's customary to call any win a team effort (and most times it will be), but much can be learned by looking at individual contributions and determining key success factors. Was there something done differently this time that had a significant impact on the final outcome? How can we capitalize on that insight and be sure it gets built into the process when we do the next project?

Positive accountability is just another way of saying that we want to model positive performance and thereby motivate all employees to invest the effort required to achieve the same level of performance. I said earlier that nothing de-energizes an employee like being anonymous in a group. Here I'll add that nothing demotivates a *good* employee like not being recognized for significant positive contributions. Where there's no accountability—negative or positive—*no* employee will be motivated to perform at a high level.

NOTICE

We also think of accountability as something that happens after the fact. But the essence of accountability is how well an individual lives up to a preset standard of behavior. Sure, if you steal a car and try to sell it to someone, you certainly knew beforehand that what you were doing was wrong. Things may not be so black and white, however, in a business setting. Is sending out a particular email a good idea, or might you be encroaching on someone else's turf? Are you allowed to have a talk with an employee about certain issues, or must you turn the matter over to Human Resources? Most businesses have strict rules about employees' communicating with the media, yet, especially in large corporations, not every employee is privy to those rules. If employees aren't familiar with the standard to which they are being held, is it fair to hold them accountable for their actions in that area?

Accountability needs to be communicated to employees beforehand. In a group setting, this means letting everyone on your team know specifically what he or she will be responsible for. In doing so, it's a good idea to put everyone's role in context so that all will appreciate the importance of their individual contributions. In preparing for a presentation, for example:

◈ The person doing the research needs to understand that the numbers collected will be used in a high-profile presentation and therefore must be the most up-to-date and accurate ones available.

◈ The person preparing the visuals needs to understand the importance of including only the most up-to-date numbers, and in creating visuals that can be easily viewed and understood.

◈ The person producing the presentation needs to understand the importance of meticulous version control.

◈ The person coordinating the event needs to be sure that the audio-visual setup is working and the speaker is easily able to navigate the presentation.

◈ The person delivering the presentation needs to tailor his or her remarks for the audience in the room.

If any person along this production line fails to execute properly the required actions for that step in the process, the entire project will fail. The best chance of seeing that every step is executed properly is to ensure that every person involved understands not only his or her role, but how that role fits into the whole process. It's a lot better to have employees who are invested in the overall project than in just one aspect of it.

INCREASING ACCOUNTABILITY

Accountability is increased when employees have notice as to what is expected of them. The more specific the expectation, the better. Also, as just described, in a group setting it helps to put everyone's role in context. This serves to get everyone invested in a team effort. Finally, never underestimate the value of a deadline. Just as some great writers and artists may be motivated primarily by a sense of mortality, people working on a project will feel a greater sense of purpose if there is a carefully defined window for their contributions. For good employees, there will be a felt need to fulfill the purpose of the project, which comes with a time requirement; for other employees, the project's purpose may be secondary to the time requirement placed on them. Whether internally or externally imposed, their accountability will be recognized.

SUMMARY

✓ System performance—whether that of a transit system or a corporation—is driven by personal performance, which in turn is driven by accountability.

✓ Compassion is not a good management strategy. It protects bad employees and demotivates good employees.

✓ Performance standards have no value if not accompanied by consequences for good or bad performance.

✓ Accountability and discipline are tools that should be used to modify substandard performance or objectionable behavior, rather than as a prelude to dismissal.

✓ Setting standards and holding individuals accountable often requires moving people to positions that are better aligned with their natural skill sets and attributes.

✓ Groups offer more and varied resources than do individuals in solving problems, but group members may be less invested in finding solutions due to increased anonymity within the group and, with it, diminished individual accountability.

✓ Accountability is also a tool for modeling positive performance. Positive[1] accountability keeps good employees motivated.

✓ Accountability is most effective when individual responsibilities are communicated to employees before a project or position begins. In a group setting, also describing how the individual's responsibilities contribute to the overall team effort will increase the individual's investment in the group's mission.

✓ Deadlines are great motivators.

CHAPTER 8

Managing Change

> Change is not a choice; don't change, and risk becoming irrelevant. A manager's primary objective in managing change is not to keep employees in their comfort zones, where there is no incentive for progress, but to communicate effectively and reduce uncertainty.

WORDS YOU MAY want to remember:

> They're quite aware of what they're going through
> Ch-ch-ch-ch-changes
> (Turn and face the strange)
> —David Bowie

This, too: We exist to facilitate, not complicate, the process of change.

Mobility is what drives economies. Cities and countries that do not invest in regional transportation are destined to lose their economic competitiveness.

Unfortunately, the United States government has never succeeded in creating a long-term funding strategy for domestic transportation. (The recently approved FAST five-year program is insufficient because, among other reasons, it lacks dedicated funding.) Several years of short-term programs in the form of continuing resolutions has left us less and less competitive internationally. In addition to the adverse macro effects of this failure, the absence of any long-term national vision or funding program has served to inhibit vision at the state and local levels.

KEEPING UP WITH CHANGE
REQUIRES . . . CHANGING

Transportation systems must evolve to remain relevant. Population and employment centers may shift over time, and, when they do, transit routes and resources must also shift to provide continuous access to them. Economic conditions change as well. Transit leaders need to be proactive in developing strategies around these changes in both internal and external environments. I remember listening to a presentation about on-time performance in routing in Chicago. The news appeared to be quite positive: On-time performance, which had been at 70 percent in the '80s, was now approaching 98 percent in the year 2000. Digging into the details, however, I learned that the ridership on one bus route had dropped from 36 passengers per revenue hour to fewer than five per hour. For this specific route, outcomes had become both highly efficient *and* incredibly ineffective. A transit system must continually monitor changes and adapt with the times to be *both* efficient and effective.

Clearly we need to change our approach to transportation—not only because of the specific requirements associated with meeting changing rider demands and expectations, but because change is a universal law. Stated simply, either embrace the gap between where you are and where you need to be and start bridging that gap . . . or become increasingly irrelevant.

All transit systems must continuously evolve and adjust to changing demographics and demands. But we see this same need for constant change in all businesses, which must evolve to remain competitive. And we see it as well at a personal level, where the extent to which we grow, learn, and change defines the richness of our lives.

CHANGE ENABLES PROGRESS

Business leaders often speak of the need to embrace change. What we really need to embrace is *progress*. The challenge we face in instituting change is getting others to recognize the *change* = *progress* relationship. Change management is likely to run up against a wall whenever that relationship is inadequately communicated.

Consider the following: In the 1960s, before I was even a twinkle in my father's eye, the U.S. government decided to change over to the metric system—gradually, over a ten-year period. The plan was that for the first five years of the changeover, any reference to a quantity, either in weight or in volume, would be given using both units of measure. The unit we were used to working with (feet, pounds, miles, pints, quarts, etc.) would come first, and the metric equivalent would follow. For the second five years, again both units of measure would be given, but now leading off with the metric unit. After 10 years, all of us would, at least in theory, be thoroughly familiar and comfortable with the metric system. The key word in the previous sentence: *theory*.

By around Year 2 or 3, apparently most people stopped paying much attention to the metric numbers, if they ever did pay any attention to them. Who wants to start talking about liters and meters when you've spent your whole life dealing with pints and quarts and feet and yards? We eventually did adopt some metric terminology—for example, the two-liter bottle of soda or the 750-milliliter bottle of wine (with which I have some familiarity)—but we still drive two miles to buy a quart of milk, and when was the last time you heard your 150-pound friend give his weight as 68 kilograms?

UNCERTAINTY—THE TRUE ENEMY OF CHANGE

The truth is, there's nothing more difficult than change. But is change really the problem? Yes, it's tempting to say (and most of us often do) that people resist change because they fear it, but is it really fear of change that causes that resistance? Isn't it more accurate to say that what people really fear and therefore resist is *uncertainty*?

Stop worrying about making your people comfortable with change. If, as a leader, you can take action to *reduce uncertainty*, your organization will be more adaptive and change will take care of itself.

People prefer what's safe and comfortable; we're always looking for ways to stay in our comfort zone. The problem is, progress doesn't happen when we stay in our comfort zone. Doesn't every great discovery start with someone being *un*comfortable?

To succeed at change management—to reduce uncertainty among your employees—you must be able to anticipate and communicate future challenges and opportunities. You must become a master of communicating *the reason* for change. How to do that effectively is a function of strategic planning, which is covered in Chapter 5. For now, I want to talk about *what* kinds of change are most achievable, and—at the heart of strategic change management—*where* change can be inserted most effectively.

WHICH TO CHANGE—
BEHAVIOR OR THOUGHT?

About 25 years ago, companies started being required to put their employees through Title VII (sex discrimination) compliance every year. Male employees who may have, up until that time, thought nothing of sharing off-color remarks with their female colleagues or even initiating casual physical contact suddenly found themselves risking dismissal because their behavior was in violation of federal law. "How can I do my best work," many wanted to know, "if I'm always worried about saying or doing the wrong thing and being dragged before the political correctness police?"

The compulsory training sessions had two basic strategies available to them: (1) Try to change thought, or (2) Forget about changing thought and just try to change behavior.

I don't have to tell you how difficult it is to change how someone thinks. It takes a lot of work over a long period of time to change someone's mind, if it can be done at all. Do you think your employees are going to change overnight their views on, for example, politics or religion? So how realistic was it for managers to expect male employees to change overnight their views on women and, related to that, how they perceived the role of women in the workplace? The fact is, people who have had a particular point of view for a long time are highly unlikely to pay much heed to any argument that would require them to adopt an opposing point of view.

The far more effective strategy, at least for Title VII compliance, was to forget about convincing anyone that all employees deserved respect, regardless of gender. Instead, new patterns of behavior were enforced through the commitment to discipline violations up to and including dismissal, the hope being that, through a process of education and enforced acclimatization over time, attitudes might eventually follow suit.

In a sense, that one is easy; there's federal law to back up the call for change. It's not quite that straightforward when it comes to other types of change in the workplace. You can't conveniently cite federal law and a government-mandated compliance program if someone resists the introduction of a new computer network or a change in job responsibilities or a new reporting system. Although behavioral change is what you're looking for, that doesn't mean you just ought to mandate new behaviors.

THE VALUE OF REASSURANCE AND EXPERIENCE

Logic alone may not work, but logic plus reassurance often does. In my experience, people will generally make their decisions emotionally and then justify them logically, so manage (or sell) accordingly. When computers first began being used for routine clerical and data management tasks in the 1970s, many employees—especially those doing administrative work—resisted, claiming that once computers came in the door, their jobs would be out the window. Arguments about the potential of computers to make their jobs more efficient often fell on deaf ears. Employees were fearful, yes, but it was a fear born not of any specific knowledge about the evils of computers but rather of uncertainty. By providing graphic (often statistical) evidence of the benefits of computers on employees' current jobs while also providing assurances that computers would actually create new and different jobs—satisfying, higher-paying jobs for which they could qualify—management was able to make its case. But it was the employees' own experience with computers—their firsthand confrontation with, and conquest of, uncertainty—that eventually led to the widespread acceptance and reliance on computers in the workplace.

Instituting change often constitutes nothing less than a frontal assault on corporate culture. *It's just not done like that around here.* How many times has a well-intentioned junior associate heard exactly those words in response to a suggestion about how to improve some process or eliminate some other kind of inefficiency? As a young technician, I heard it plenty. It was like a punch in the gut, but I was just stupid enough to keep getting up.

CHANGING A CULTURE—
A TRUE STORY

As a manager, I've worked in a number of regressive environments. In some, it was the union's resistance to change that was at the root of the problem, but this is certainly not a problem specific to unions, nor are all unions change-averse. Some quick background: I grew up in a union household and was a union technician at the beginning of my career. I appreciate that many of the benefits that employees enjoy today were fought for and won by unions that had the courage to face down oppressive owners and managers. But I have also experienced environments in which weak union leadership has had a decidedly adverse impact on job security. I also believe that unions, in one form or another, will be more relevant in the future. As inherited wealth becomes more prominent, people who have never earned a dime in their lives will acquire fortunes and be responsible for organizations that are made successful by working-class people. Ever growing, the gap between spoiled wealth and the working class will require some level of representation to maintain a reasonable exchange of work for pay. But for now, back to some old realities.

In 1998 I was in charge of three large SEPTA divisions in Philadelphia. The largest—the Berridge facility—was responsible for rebuilding engines and transmissions and vehicle overhaul. In short, our technicians would completely tear down a bus and rebuild it to "like new" condition. Following a third-party assessment, executive leadership charged me, newly assigned to this position, to make immediate and lasting changes in the facility's operations.

The union leadership was opposed to any change and filed dozens of grievances every day for purely nuisance reasons. There were about 15 of these leaders who called themselves the "shirt gang" because they wore the same color shirts every day (blue on Monday, red on Tuesday, etc.) as a sign of unity. They intimidated any employee who didn't follow their rules on the floor. This had been going on for several years prior to my arrival. If you were looking for a great example of what can happen in a work environment that has a leadership vacuum, one day at Berridge and your search would be over.

In March 1998, with the union contract set to expire, tensions were unusually high. Executive management asked that two buses be painted without any SEPTA livery so that they could be used for security in the event of a work stoppage. When union leadership was tipped off as to the purpose of these "special buses," a few rogue employees vandalized them by destroying and disabling the electronic engine control module (ECM).

When I called the union section officer onto one of the buses that was vandalized and let him know what had happened, he laughed at me, claiming that his members would never do anything like that. He smiled and winked at me as he walked off the bus.

I stayed late that night with a few technicians who replaced the damaged control module and prepared the two buses for security detail. A replacement ECM cost $2,500 plus labor.

A few days after the contract expired and the parties agreed to continue talks without a work stoppage, the union section officer, upon his return to work, came to my office to tell me that the union filing cabinet had been broken into and 30 years' worth of union records were missing. He said that the files contained financial records, hearing notes, and confidential documents. I suggested to him that it must have been the same group that vandalized the buses on Friday and assured him that I would report the incident to the police. Still, I could not resist the temptation to smile and wink as he left my office. Change was going to happen here, come what may.

In 2002—four years after change came to the Berridge facility—the benefits of change had become dramatically clear. People touring the facility as part of the American Public Transportation Association (APTA) International Conference openly commented on the fine organization of work, the meticulously clean facility, and the high morale of the workforce. Managers and technicians alike were proud of what we had accomplished. After all, it was just a few years earlier that things had been so out of control. Managers appearing on the shop floor had been greeted with synchronized obscenities or hammer pounding on benches, which was designed to deter managers from walking the floor, as well as warn others sitting on buses or sleeping in work areas to awaken before getting caught. Employees who were capable of far better production but were unwilling to accept the abuse attached to working efficiently had felt compelled to slow their output. Workers exceeding production levels set by the controlling groups were issued stern warnings. A dead rat on your workbench, industrial-strength super glue in your toolbox lock, and chassis grease in your clothes locker were all methods of intimidation used to deter any appearance of cooperative effort between employees and SEPTA management. And managers felt helpless to try to stop this. Any attempt to crack down on an employee for violating rules was met with personal threats of revenge.

In November 1997, managers collectively made a decision to change the social contract at this facility. Although the labor agreement was an obstacle to workplace communication between managers and employees, nothing could stop managers from communicating with individuals on a personal level. Behind closed doors, union members acknowledged the need for change but, with few exceptions, were reluctant to demonstrate openly anything resembling cooperation. So we started with some basic steps: communicating with the workforce at daily and monthly group meetings, conveying clear and reasonable expectations, removing the walls that had been erected between workstations, conducting interviews and administering accountability for employees violating rules, and, most important, having managers spend time on the floor. People who cared told us what had to be changed and even recommended ways to help us in the process.

I met with union representatives at various levels to discuss the need for change. I asked for their support in getting it done, but that support never came. They themselves felt threatened. In January 1998, using input from numerous individuals on the shop floor, a group of managers drafted and distributed a strategic business plan. A vocal minority in the shop, supported by several members of union staff, initiated a campaign to undermine the process. They spread misinformation and threatened managers at all levels, myself included. After discovering a brick with an attached threat on my front lawn, I rearranged my schedule to police my property before going to work so that my wife and kids wouldn't have to read words unfit for human consumption. Other managers faced the same sort of harassment: Pictures of our homes would be sent via mail addressed to our families with notes attached that said "We're watching you" or words to that effect. Advising union officials of these and other attempts at intimidation (such as pornographic pictures being sent to our wives) only meant more mail and more threats.

Our only response was to spend more time on the floor, and more time with people who cared. In February 1998, closed-circuit television was installed throughout the facility to provide further help in monitoring the workplace. We were determined to involve people in the process, protect them from intimidation, provide resources, and hold them accountable.

A key component of our eventual success was transparency. Process evaluation now had the involvement of everyone who conducted the work and was involved with the process—production control, management, and union officials. A process evaluation was nothing more than monitoring the work within its own environment. That is to say, we would observe people conducting the work and report on what was required in terms of safety, tooling, and process, as well as the time required to perform the process, all of which resulted in a basis for accountability (not to mention tremendous savings for the taxpayers funding the public process). An evaluation of one engine line process produced labor savings of $1,215 per vehicle. Extrapolating from that gave us savings of $4,860 per week and approximately $250,000 per year for one job process (and there were thousands of work processes), allowing the facility to do more with less without compromising the final product.

CHANGING CULTURE—
AN ANALYSIS

Figure 8 is an attempt to summarize the process by which change happens in an organization. What it also depicts is the cycle of beliefs that are burned into the "cultural psyche" of an organization or a person in that organization.

Beliefs drive actions, actions produce results, and results create experiences. That sounds fine, except that, as discussed earlier, it's nearly impossible to change what someone believes. What a manager can and should focus on is creating new experiences. These new experiences foster new beliefs, which in turn create new actions and, with them, different results. Beliefs do not change without experiences changing them. When leadership focuses on experiences, change acceleration occurs. Whether this occurs within a positive cycle or a negative cycle is a choice that leadership must make.

What a manager can and should focus on is creating new experiences.

Beliefs do not change without experiences changing them.

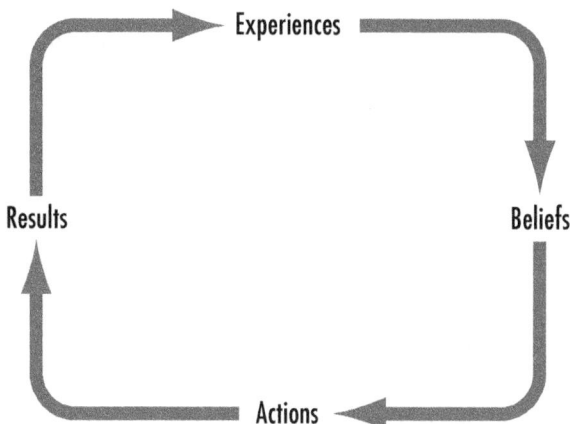

Figure 8. The process of change and the cycle of beliefs.

Managing change is about managing organizational conflict and culture. Change can take many forms, including:

◇ A new management structure.
◇ A new strategic direction.
◇ The use of new technology.
◇ Changes in the economy that necessitate cost-cutting measures.
◇ New government regulations.
◇ A new competitor or other changes in the marketplace.
◇ Perhaps just a general shift in consumer preferences brought about by any number of factors.

In every case, business survival requires moving quickly to give employees the experiences and assurances that will minimize uncertainty and maintain (or increase) motivation. The other side of business survival is the need to keep customers (as opposed to employees) in *their* comfort zone even while process changes affect the delivery of products and services to them. But why, you may ask, is that necessary . . . assuming that all changes are designed to benefit customers? Well, renovations are designed to increase the value of a home and the quality of life of those residing in it, but have you ever lived through a renovation? To repeat what I said earlier: *There's nothing more difficult than change.*

SUMMARY

✓ The world is continuously changing. To remain relevant, organizations must change along with it.
✓ Resistance to change comes not from fear of change as much as it comes from uncertainty. Reducing uncertainty leads to a more adaptive organization.

✓ Managing change dose not mean keeping employees in their comfort zone. A comfort zone is not a conducive venue for progress.

✓ Change is easier to achieve when employees are reassured as to its benefits and able to experience the new process or application themselves.

✓ Managing change should focus on creating new experiences, which in turn foster new beliefs and actions.

✓ Managing change, in whatever form that change takes, goes right to the heart of organizational conflict and culture.

CHAPTER 9

Social and Business Equity

We go through life with a ledger hanging over us. On one side are all of the good things we've done, the contributions we've made to a better world, whether we gave more than we got. On the other side are the things that were given to us that we may not have paid for—financially, intellectually, and emotionally. In business, leadership comes from building positive equity with employees, customers, and colleagues. Life is a system of credits and debits, and, especially in the end, it's best not to be overdrawn.

EQUITY. IT's A word that means different things to different people. For many people, the word "equity" triggers thoughts of home ownership and the benefits of being able to use your home as collateral to borrow against its value. The equity you have in an asset is defined as the difference between what you owe and the market value of that asset. Lenders will usually allow you to borrow against this difference. There are many parallels in life.

The equity you have in an asset is the difference between what you owe and the market value of that asset.

EQUITY BASICS

When people talk about karma, what they're really talking about is equity. Good karma = positive equity; bad karma = negative equity. For those less inclined to use spiritual terminology to describe such matters, you can think of equity as being analogous to a balance of trade. When a country exports more than it imports, it is said to have a positive balance of trade. Import more than you export, and you have a negative balance of trade. We can talk about positive or negative imbalance in just about every facet of our lives, even in our relationship to ourselves. Consider:

◆ *Our minds:* Do we contribute in a meaningful way to the preservation of mental acuity? Are we reading only information that supports our long-held belief systems or do we read opposing or disagreeable information to gain a broader perspective or understanding? Are we always learning, or have we given up on trying to challenge and thereby improve our minds?

◆ *Our bodies:* Do we eat correctly? Do we exercise? Do we take safety precautions or unnecessary risks?

◆ *Our souls:* Do we attend to our spiritual development, either religious or nonreligious? Do we practice positive thinking (for example, with affirmations) or do we dwell on the unfortunate and unpleasant events in our lives?

◆ *Our social lives:* Do we spend time with friends? Do we have access to a support system in the event of misfortune? What are we doing to contribute to our communities?

Equity is about reciprocity. Are we proactive or reactive? Do we give before we take, or do we take before we give? Is our balance positive or negative?

Equity is of special importance in personal relationships. There is a give and take to any relationship. Give more than you take and you will have achieved positive relational equity. One caveat: In a relationship, this gap between contribution and receipt should not be seen as a debt waiting to be repaid. Looking at a romantic relationship in strictly financial terms is never a good idea. I will go only so far as to say that my wife and I have been together for almost 30 years, in part because both of us rely on a positive balance of equity to get us through the bad arguments and tough times. When you make time for good, meaningful contributions in a relationship, you create equity and time. Having no equity—or only negative equity—in a personal relationship magnifies difficulties. How is negative equity created? That's easy: Just treat someone badly, don't listen, don't share, take no interest in another person's life, betray a trust, be rude, be inconsiderate, etc.

EQUITY IN THE WORKPLACE

In your place of employment, you contribute to work both as an individual and as part of a collective. An executive in any organization earns loyalty with positive equity. When people apply minimal effort and simply go through the motions, the absence of positive equity is often the reason. You can buy a person's back—you cannot buy his heart and soul.

Leadership is about providing the positive equity that moves people to contribute discretionary effort. No equity = no extra effort. Welcome to life on the shop floor. As a technician in Philadelphia, I saw firsthand how good managers get so much more from the same employees than bad managers do. I felt good when I was trusted, involved, and knew expectations. Managers develop equity when they are inclusive.

Managers develop equity when they are inclusive.

Over the course of my career I have witnessed, many more times than I care to remember, the attempts of well-educated, well-intentioned managers to drive good people to better performance by pushing them harder. To no one's surprise—no one other than those managers, anyway—performance suffered. A couple of simple truths: (1) People respond to mismanagement by getting even; (2) Good employees are especially good at getting even. Managers with negative equity lose big in this transaction, and their organizations generally pay the price. This doesn't mean that, as a manager, you need to be agreeable or even pleasant (although there's really no harm in that). It means that you need to be fair and inclusive and open to other points of view.

When I was negotiating contracts with the Amalgamated Transit Union (ATU) in Albany, I often got into lengthy conversations with the ATU president about compensation. I wanted to pay our workforce at a wage that was competitive for the region and the occupation they held. The president would often tell me that I didn't understand what people should earn because I was making an executive salary. I would reply that I didn't concern myself with what I made when I was servicing buses at $8.63 an hour. I focused on doing my job and improving my skills (developing equity) and maybe that's why I was now making what I was making. Both in Philadelphia and in Albany, negotiations with the union would often result in language that was favorable to the most senior drivers and mechanics at the expense of younger talent. In Albany, driver retention was a major issue for us. Drivers would start work, go through training, get their commercial driver's license, and then leave for higher pay. The issue wasn't that our top driver wages weren't competitive; it was that our starting wage was too low and it took five years for someone to get to full wage.

During negotiations with the ATU in 2007, I cut progression from five to three years, increased the starting wage, and developed an accelerated progression program in which an employee with good work habits (attendance, customer service, and performance) could reach full wage in less time.

All of this was positive . . . except that the union, when left alone, will often "eat its young." At the end of a two-year stalemate, the union said it was ready to advance the contract to a vote. The only catch: The union wanted me to take the money that was allocated for the change in progression and use it to increase top wages for the existing operators. And the guys just starting off? Well, you could forget about them. So I refused. Yes, it took a bit longer, but the contract eventually went forward with the changed starting wages and progression, and the organization and I had established equity with people I had yet to meet.

SWEAT EQUITY

When you hear the term "sweat equity," you probably picture someone doing some kind of manual labor, such as carpentry or painting, rather than writing a check to a carpenter or painter to do the work. We may think of sweat equity as that which results from other than financial investment, but "sweat equity" can be used to describe just about any investment of time where there is no expectation of immediate benefit. When your contributions are one-dimensional, you're developing sweat equity. A young mind perfecting a trade, an athlete spending additional hours to improve performance, someone attending college—all are investing sweat equity into their future lives. They are working to maximize what could become a future opportunity but with no guarantee of any return on their investment.

When I was a young diesel technician–3rd class, I absorbed information like a sponge. I would work long hours and, even with a young family at home, manage to spend time at the library reading about a technical subject related to my field. I couldn't learn fast enough. I was making only $10.75 per hour and this sweat equity wasn't earning me an extra nickel over and above that in the form of hourly compensation or bonus, but I knew I was building equity in my future.

BUSINESS EQUITY WITH THE COMMUNITY

Reduced to its simplest terms, the effectiveness of board governance is gauged by assessing the relationship that exists between the organization and its authorizing environment—namely the constituents served by the organization. In a transit system, this would include the state and county legislature, taxpayers, transit riders, and the communities that are served. As CEO in Albany I would spend a significant amount of my time in the community, riding buses and meeting with groups to gain a better understanding of a variety of topics, including riders' views on issues related to mobility, connections, and what really mattered to them. This face-to-face contact with the community was especially important in the planning phase of a new project, such as the rebuilding of a rail station or the planning of a new bus service.

Each time a discussion was held either individually or collectively, I would build equity in the business relationship between the community and my board of directors. Just the fact of our meeting was often enough to get things started on the right track. After all, inclusion creates equity, as does listening. (Contrast that with exclusion, which creates apathy and distrust.) Action, on the other hand, can both create and destroy equity. There will always be those who prefer no action or who are opposed to the project (and, with it, progress) that you're about to initiate. The goal is to have more positive than negative equity with your constituents so as not to get ahead of your downfield blocking when you do take action.

BUSINESS EQUITY WITH THE CUSTOMER

There's nothing mysterious about how to build relational equity with stakeholders at the customer level. A student guide from Sales 101 will tell you pretty much all you need to know. Have a good product, spend time learning the issues facing your customer in deciding whether to purchase your product, have good support systems in place after the sale, and show your customer appreciation for the sale.

Sales managers will often note their concerns when a customer calls with an issue or service claim. Although nobody likes to hear about a premature failure or an issue with a product that you manufacture, I really can't think of a better time to build personal and business equity with key accounts and customers. Most customers are reasonable and understand that, on occasion, things go wrong. It's how we respond to those issues and concerns that develops and maintains positive equity. Every challenge is an opportunity to create or destroy equity.

POSITIONAL EQUITY IN AN ORGANIZATION

Here's a hard truth for you: When you're new to a position, you have no equity. That's because you haven't contributed or accomplished anything for the benefit of the organization. Over time you will develop skill sets and make contributions to the organization (positive equity), as well as withdraw some benefit from what the organization can offer to you (negative equity), depending on your individual performance within the organization. A good quarter, half, or year in sales on your part will help you weather a bad quarter somewhere down the line because you now have "positional equity." In other words, you have made a positive contribution and have standing to explain a downturn.

It's a lot more difficult when you cannot point to a good quarter and have only a series of bad quarters on your résumé; there's no equity to absorb the loss in the event of another bad quarter. I have been involved in literally hundreds of disciplinary hearings and have always favored mitigating discipline for employees with positional equity. That is to say, I would never treat a 20-year employee with minimal issues the same as I would treat a two-year employee with multiple infractions. For the former, I would reduce or "hold discipline in abeyance"; for the latter, I would accelerate discipline.

INTERGENERATIONAL EQUITY

Intergenerational equity refers to the funding of today's assets without ignoring the need that additional funding will be needed tomorrow. For example, in many cases transit systems today will attempt to front the entire cost of capital. Instead, transit systems using public funds should be forced to pay for this capital, especially assets with useful lives extending beyond a decade over the time that they are deployed. Leasing or debt service plans can be used to structure terms. Another example is education. Young students should be eligible to receive government-subsidized, minimal-interest loans that can be repaid over their careers.

It has been said that you can judge a nation by how well it takes care of its elderly. This is simply a recognition of intergenerational equity. The men and women who have paved the roads (literally and figuratively) for today's generation have positive equity with respect to the younger men and women who use those roads.

In the United States today, banks are able to borrow money from the federal government at one percent interest, and have been enjoying extremely low interest rates for a very long time. The rationale for subsidizing loans to financial institutions is easy to understand: Access to capital encourages spending and thus creates employment. That said, isn't access to education good for our children and good for our country? A well-educated younger generation is a competitive advantage for any country in a global economy. In the United States, we don't limit education to what we (the older generation) know. We teach kids how to think, how to process new information, and, ultimately, how to create a future of their own that extends the boundaries of anything that we were able to create. So why not subsidize college loans at the same level that bank loans are subsidized? Acccss to low-interest loans for education creates equity between today and tomorrow. It is paying today for a better future!

APPLIED EQUITY

All parents want to give their kids more than they themselves had growing up. Unfortunately, this unwritten rule is becoming increasingly difficult to satisfy. I also believe that the greatest gift you can give your children is independence. Balancing those two—independence and a better future—can sometimes mean walking a fine line. Yes, I'm blessed with the ability to pay for my children's college education, but I think there's also room for reason. That's why they all get the same deal: Graduate with a 3.2 GPA or higher, and I pay the bill; anything lower and you get to repay the loan. The message is clear: I will not fund your party. There's no free lunch or, in life, anything free that's of any value. Value requires effort. It's a good connection to establish early in life.

LIFE EQUITY

And finally there's life equity. No biggie here—it's just having your whole life evaluated right at the end, based on one simple question: Did you give more than you got? Think of that final graveyard scene in "Saving Private Ryan": *Was I a good man? Did I lead a good life?* Was there ever a more emotionally wrenching scene anywhere?

Every life is an equity gauge. I believe that our lives are evaluated according to how we use what we've been given to help improve the world. Do we give more than we take? Include more than we extract? Love more than we hate? Did we help others more than others helped us? Did we contribute more than we consumed? And did we leave the world better or worse that we found it?

Every day I wake up and ask myself the same question: What am I going to contribute today to my employer, my organization, my family, and my community? What can I give today?

SUMMARY

✓ Equity is analogous to a balance of trade. Export more than you import and you have a positive balance of trade. Give more than you receive and you have positive equity.

✓ Every facet of our lives—our mind, body, spirituality, and social life—can be described in terms of a positive or negative imbalance.

✓ Leadership requires providing the positive equity that moves people to go the extra mile.

✓ "Sweat equity" describes an investment of time to maximize a potential opportunity but with no guarantee of any return.

✓ Inclusion and listening create equity. Action can both create and destroy equity. A positive balance of equity helps in placating—and perhaps even winning over—those who prefer that no action be taken.

✓ Basic sales skills are all that's needed to build relational equity with stakeholders at the customer level.

✓ Positional equity refers to one's having made past contributions to an organization (through, for example, sales performance) sufficient to "get a pass" on a bad quarter here and there.

✓ Intergenerational equity refers to the repayment of today's negative equity over the course of the future use of those assets—for example, the government subsidization of low-interest student loans.

✓ Every life is an equity gauge. Do we give more than we take? Is the world a better place because we were here?

Afterword

I SUPPOSE THAT ANYONE reading this book could easily conclude that it's a book about transportation. Confession: I *have* talked a lot about transportation in these pages, but that's not because I want to emphasize my knowledge of trains and buses. It's because I'm convinced that there are many parallels between running a transit system and succeeding at life.

If you want to get to where you're going—in a transit system, in a business, or in your personal life—you need to plan your trip. Bumper-sticker wisdom for those wishing to succeed:

> *Every trip starts with a plan.*
> *Every plan starts with a vision.*

You wouldn't construct a transit system without first determining where prospective riders needed to go. As one of those riders, you wouldn't buy a ticket and get on a train without first determining the best route to your destination. Likewise, in life (no matter what your age) it's always a good idea to think about your destination.

In every case, the journey or the project (which is certainly a journey of sorts) begins with a vision. Admittedly, envisioning the transfer points on a transit system isn't exactly the Vision of Bernadette, but it's the kind of imagining you need to do to design a system that serves a useful purpose.

Purpose, like vision, is another word that appears more than a few times in the preceding pages. The distinction I hoped to draw was that a purpose is what you do for your customers, while a vision is what you want to do for them in the future (and which presumably is more than what you're doing for them today). An organization must be built around a purpose before it can grow to realize a vision. In every successful business, organizational configuration is consistent with the business's purpose and its need for effective communication.

It was also important to me to spend a good bit of time talking about making connections, managing choices rather than time, and setting standards against which to be measured and for which to be held accountable. In transportation, in business, and in one's personal life, not much is going to be accomplished unless those three activities are part of the plan.

Back to the plan. It's what brings vision to life—what makes it more than just a dream or an item on a wish list. If designed and executed effectively, it's what takes a transit system or a business or an individual from initial purpose to future destination.

A strategic plan is the bridge that links vision and action. As we've seen, a good plan takes into account a whole range of factors that go well beyond what the individual or organization can bring to bear by way of resources, personal or otherwise, in capturing the vision within a series of discrete action steps. A good plan also evolves as needed to account for external variables—political, economic, social, and technological—that may make the original plan untenable. It realistically reflects the internal strengths and weaknesses available for confronting identified external opportunities and threats.

I also talked about the need to execute a plan if it is to have any value, and how the skills required for successful execution are not the same as those required in a planning position. Planning is often a solitary activity, primarily carried out by a small group of people locked in a room. Execution is more outwardly focused; it requires securing the active support of stakeholders and employees, as well as finding someone with the appropriate authority to champion the plan.

My inclusion of all of those transit system anecdotes was intended to reveal a bias of mine: The resistance to change on the part of employees (and particularly those in unions) is almost always the toughest obstacle to putting a strategic plan into practice. The good news is that resistance to change comes not from fear but from uncertainty. So be inclusive, be transparent, be reassuring, but, at the same time, be clear: Change is going to happen, and everyone is responsible for contributing to the successful transition to a new way of doing things. I never expected people to embrace change; what I wanted them to embrace was *progress*.

In spite of the many books written on the subject of planning and execution and change management and time management and all of the other challenges in business and in life that we face every day, in the end we're left to ask ourselves the same basic questions: Putting aside whatever material rewards have been involved, what have we really achieved in our work and in our lives? Have we given more than we've received? And, as leaders, have we given enough to move our people to ask those same questions?

It is my deepest hope that this book has provided you with a workable framework within which to analyze your own leadership approach—a framework that will stimulate new ideas as you seek solutions to the challenges you face at work and in every other facet of your life.

www.ingramcontent.com/pod-product-compliance
Lightning Source LLC
Chambersburg PA
CBHW021100210326
41598CB00016B/1270